Delight Sweetser

One Way Round the World

Delight Sweetser

One Way Round the World

ISBN/EAN: 9783744722117

Printed in Europe, USA, Canada, Australia, Japan

Cover: Foto ©Andreas Hilbeck / pixelio.de

More available books at **www.hansebooks.com**

A GEISHA

*One Way Round the World:
By Delight Sweetser : With
Illustrations from Photographs*

Second Edition

Indianapolis—Kansas City
The Bowen-Merrill Company
MDCCCXCIX

To my
Father and Mother
and all others whose companionship
made of
this journey a delightful
memory

TABLE OF CONTENTS

I
Car Window Reflections 1

II
On the Pathless Pacific 8

III
The Islands of the Pacific 17

IV
In Yokohama 30

V
Japanese Customs and Beliefs 39

VI
Tokio and Elsewhere 48

VII
The Mikado's Birthday 57

VIII
Japan's Glorious Mountains 71

IX
Odds and Ends 83

X
In Palace, Temple and Theater 93

XI
In Old Shanghai 102

XII
A Week in Wen Chow, China 112

Table of Contents

XIII
In the China Sea 119

XIV
In Canton 126

XV
From Hong-Kong to Singapore 134

XVI
The Land of Gems and Flowers 145

XVII
What we Saw in India 160

XVIII
A Glimpse of the Ganges 172

XIX
Benares, the Holy City of India 184

XX
A Wise Man of India 192

XXI
Agra and its Taj Mahal 200

XXII
A Modern Prince of India 213

XXIII
In Egypt 229

XXIV
In the Shadow of the Pyramids 245

XXV
Due West Again 258

LIST OF ILLUSTRATIONS

A GEISHA	*Frontispiece*
FIRST GLIMPSE OF THE PARADISE OF THE PACIFIC	16
THE GARDEN OF THE ARLINGTON, HONOLULU	20
ON THE LAVA BED	28
MISS MOONSHINE, MISS PERFUME AND MISS CHERRY BLOSSOM	30
JAPANESE JUNKS	32
A JAPANESE LADY IN HER JINRIKISHA	34
TEMPLE ENTRANCE AT NIKKO	40
JAPANESE GIRLS	44
THE MONKEYS AT NIKKO	48
AN APPROVED JAPANESE MACKINTOSH	54
FUJI IN CHRYSANTHEMUMS	56
THE PAGODA AT NIKKO	60
A GARDEN IN TOKYO	70
DRUM AND SAMISEN PLAYERS	78
TAKING CARE OF THE BABY	80
SACRED DANCERS AT NARA	82
JAPANESE WORKMEN	84
A TEMPLE	86
A SIGN IN TOKYO	90
THE ENTRANCE OF A THEATER	94
A THEATER STREET	98
A SHANGHAI CAB	102
CHINESE ACTORS	106
A CHINESE FAMILY OF WEALTH	110
CHINESE COFFINS AWAITING BURIAL	112
CHINESE JUNK, SHOWING THE EYE	122
SAMPANS AT CANTON	126
AN ORIENTAL COSTUME	138

Illustrations

BY JINRIKISHA IN SINGAPORE	142
WOMAN OF CEYLON	144
A "JOLLY" BOAT	146
SNAKE CHARMER AND JUGGLER	148
A SINGHALESE GROUP	150
NATIVE BUNGALOWS NEAR KANDY	152
THE TEMPLE OF THE TOOTH	154
AN ELEPHANT AT WORK	156
GIANT BAMBOO	158
DEVIL DANCERS OF CEYLON	162
ON THE WAY TO DARJEELING	178
BRAHMIN WORSHIPING	186
ON THE BANKS OF THE GANGES AT BENARES	188
A LITTLE TAMIL BRIDE	190
HOLY MAN OF BENARES	192
AN ASCETIC	194
BURNING GHAT AT BENARES	196
PAVILION AT LUCKNOW	198
BULLOCK CART, LUCKNOW	202
DOMES OF THE PEARL MOSQUE, AGRA	206
PIERCED MARBLE SCREENS AT AGRA	208
ARCHES IN THE PEARL MOSQUE	210
THE TAJ MAHAL	212
THE FORT AT DELHI	220
TOMBS IN OLD DELHI	222
A ZENANA CART	224
SAIS	236
BACKSHEESH, "LEDDY"	238
DAHABEAHS ON THE NILE	248
CAIRO, FROM THE CITADEL	252
A FAIR CAIRENE	254
SUEZ CANAL	260
ONE OF LANDSEER'S LIONS	268

One Way Round the World

I

Car Window Reflections

"EAST or west, home's best," so they say and so it is, and I find a little rust of regret on the fine edge of my enthusiasm to think that my path back to Hoosierdom lies over some forty thousand odd miles and around the globe. Like the old lady who said she was glad to get back but sorry to return, I am glad to start but sorry to go. However, I have started for Indiana, if by a truly roundabout way. Rapid transit threatens to make all the world alike, in a century or two, and I call myself fortunate to see the lands of fans and rat tails before Madame Chrysanthemum rides the bicycle or Mr. Ah Sin introduces the trolley party.

. . . .

What a varied and often brilliant series of pictures my car window has framed for me on my long journey overland. Corn! Corn! Corn! in Kansas, enough to feed the world one would think, stretching away in waving golden fields to meet the blue horizon. Wide, treeless stretches of tableland in Colorado, a sky every whit as blue as Italy's, clear and cloudless, with a fringe of misty mountains. A veritable garden of Eden in the Salt Lake Valley, reclaimed from the desert by the thrifty Mormons. Nevada—sage brush, sand and desolation;

One Way Round the World

a sombre veneer for the shining metals that lie hidden in its bosom. And then California, introduced by the wild, wooded slopes of the Sierra Nevada, by magnificent peaks and deep cut canons; afterward, gay and smiling and flowery, a delight to the eye.

Seeing is believing the beauty of mountain scenery. Neither an author's pen nor an artist's brush can more than suggest the vivid reality. Stories in dialect and descriptions of scenery were ever unpardonable to me, and let the man who never sees mountains live a joyous life in the plains, undisturbed by being told about them. An hour's stroll in the shops of Colorado Springs is a good object lesson in what to avoid, a striking illustration of what ugly things money will buy. An air of untidiness and worse pervades the place and it is out of doors that one must look for the beauty that has made it famous. The Garden of the Gods is a really beautiful spot, with a wealth of color and an astonishing number of odd-shaped rocks, astonishingly named. I made the same discovery in Colorado Springs that M. Alphonse Daudet did in London—that it is silent! There is great activity in the streets, too; but it is withal noiseless and dreamy and restful. Perhaps the fine air that blows off mountain slopes is responsible for the impression.

Everything is done there under the auspices of Pike's Peak. At every turn one's eye rests on that grand old mountain. There is something singularly masculine about its gaunt slopes and massive peak, just as some of the more delicate of the Alpine peaks suggest femininity. The Rockies can never be rivals of the Alps unless it is in the actual and uninteresting number of feet that they tower above sea level. In this more southerly latitude the snow line is too high, the valleys too broad, the whole surrounding plateau too elevated to give that magnificent effect of height and grandeur so often seen in Switzerland. Yet there is a great charm of color, of hazy atmosphere, of light and shade. The ride from Colorado Springs to Glenwood is a marvelous one, crowned by one of the greatest feats of American engineering, the tunnel of the Hagerman pass, a two-mile tunnel that cost a million and a half dollars to build. After a toilsome climb of hours behind two puffing, straining engines, the train pierces the mountains, crosses the "divide" and literally coasts down to Glenwood without an ounce of steam, falling five thousand feet in sixty-five miles. The names of the little mountain settlements, by courtesy called towns, have a mellow Colorado flavor — Rifle, Cellar, Parachute, Peachblow, Frying Pan, etc.

If I might be permitted to coin a phrase for our language, I would suggest "the tame and cottony East." There might be some difficulty in defining its boundaries, as the San Francisco man goes "East" to Salt Lake, and some New Yorkers go West to Buffalo. However that may be, the effrontery of the individual who called the West wild and woolly has long rankled in my soul. If we are wild, is he not tame? If we are woolly, why is he not cottony? Yet there is no denying that the West is very ragged; very Oshkosh, as it were. A Rocky Mountain town is a "specimen" not to be

One Way Round the World

found elsewhere, well set in cheerless surroundings. A side track, a saloon, a general store, a dozen shanties, a painted house that belongs to the nabob of the settlement, a dispirited tree or two, an unlimited background and sideground and foreground of sage brush and sand —of such is the far western town.

. . . .

Perhaps there is no more fruitful field for the study of "types" than the overland train. The young and the old, the intellectual and the ignorant, he who has been rich, or is, or will be, all fraternize surprisingly. A little company of souls whose lives are tangent at one point, who eat, drink, and are merry together and whose paths lie in as many directions as the wind's.

The Pullman palace cars are not all the name suggests. Perhaps the pioneer, who crossed in '58, when Denver was seven days by stage from Quincy, Illinois, would not be so captious a critic, but the majority of end-of-the-century travelers are apt to agree with the man who said he hated to pay such a high price for insomnia. At night the sleeper accumulates such a load of dust and cinders that an early morning riser, if a man, is apt to be mistaken for the porter. He, however, has a fair chance of rectifying the mistake, but when the new-woman porter arrives, the women passengers may have to resort to badges for distinction.

Why a man, who has about half the number of garments to put on that a woman has, should be allotted double the space for a dressing and washing room, is a question that might be referred to the sphinx—or Mr.

Car Window Reflections

Pullman. The fact that a man is, sometimes, twice as big as a woman, isn't consoling in the least, and as a last straw, man is given a smoking room beside. It has always seemed amusing to me that it is in the United States, where woman has the greatest privileges and the most enviable position, that she howls the loudest for her rights, but this *affaire de Pullman* is enough to engender rebellion in the meekest heart.

Among the passengers leaving Colorado Springs was a jolly party of four, easily known as southerners by their accent. I amused myself by surmising the relations of the quartet and their probable destination, for they had a vast amount of impedimenta in the way of guns and rods. Two of them I disposed of as husband and wife, the other two as brother and sister, the sister being, according to such reckoning, a jolly old maid. The only ray of consolation that came to me afterward was that I had rightly guessed that the party was going bear hunting in the Rockies, for the jolly old maid told me that she and her husband were taking their "second wedding trip," to celebrate the birth of their first grandchild, and that she was the mother of ten children, five boys and five girls. Really, I think that was the most ponderous misfit that I ever devised.

. . . .

As in the old days all roads led to Rome, so all California roads apparently lead to San Francisco.

San Francisco itself, with its slanting streets, handsome buildings, beautiful views and flowery gardens has a great charm. It is known all over the state as

One Way Round the World

"the city," and often referred to ambiguously as "down below." The expression was probably coined by some tenderfoot who had been slid up and down some of its amazing hills on the cable cars. Necessity is truly the mother of invention and it is in San Francisco that the cable system was introduced and in San Francisco that it is most nearly perfected. Even under such difficulties as the hills offer, the cars run very smoothly. The inclines are so steep that it is something of a novelty to ride in a cable car without feeling that you are in immediate danger of dislocating most anything.

In San Francisco, the upper ten most appropriately live on Nob Hill, away up at the tip top of California street. It is an imposing site for fine mansions. They tower majestically over the city in the day time and twinkle with starry lights at night. Almost all of these buildings are of wood, the danger of earthquakes being always in people's minds.

We have seen the stock sights of the city, Sutro Heights, and Baths, the Seal Rocks, Cliff House, etc., but the most of San Francisco and California must be left for another time. A peep at Chinatown was interesting, and we can some day compare it with a real China town. The red and yellow and purple and blue little folks, with their odd, little, one-sided pig-tails, were the most entertaining. A delicious little Celestial, yellow and almond-eyed, dressed in all the colors of the rainbow, gave my finger a tight squeeze, just as an American baby would have done.

Car Window Reflections

Kathryn Kidder is at the Baldwin in Madame Sans-Gêne. The play is pleasing but not to be compared with the French production. Miss Kidder's conception of the character of Madame Sans-Gêne, the washerwoman who becomes the duchess, has little of the exquisite delicacy and pathos with which Réjane's shines. The audience was fashionable, but we had a very bad case of the man who laughs in the wrong place, just behind us. Of the individuals we long to miss, he heads the list.

. . . .

Among my traveling companions going over to Oakland one day were two strikingly beautiful girls, who linger in my memory. One was plainly of the people, brilliant in complexion, innocent in expression, faultless in form and feature. The other, chic, refined, elegant, had a beautiful, intelligent face, with a faint, fascinating frown across her perfect brow. My eyes were irresistibly drawn to one or the other of those bewitching faces. They have an association of native sons in this state, sons born on the soil, and I wondered if these were native daughters. One might sigh to be a Californian if all were such. I was reminded that three women, all famous for their wit and intellect, were once asked if they would rather be brilliant or beautiful and they all replied unhesitatingly, "Beautiful."

There is food for further reflections.

II

On the Pathless Pacific

AT four P. M. on September twenty-first, the good ship "City of Peking" steamed through the Golden Gate for still another of her long voyages on the pathless Pacific. The hosts of preparations that each one of us represented were all finished, the last good-bye had been waved, the broad sea lay before us and we were left to practice the art, as Artemus Ward put it, of "keeping inside your berth and outside your dinner."

There is something very dramatic about the sailing of a great ocean vessel, something almost sad, a picture that frames itself in memory but eludes the pen when one tries to put it into words. As the moment of our departure draws near, a contagious excitement fills the air. All the passengers are warned to make haste to come on board and the visitors warned to land by a pig-tailed Celestial, who vigorously hammers a deafening gong. There is a tremendous bustle among the people on the dock. The crowd of friends who come to wave *bon voyage* repeat for the hundredth time to "be sure and write"; many eyes glisten suspiciously, jokes on seasickness flourish, belated baggage arrives in rumbling wagons, the officers shout orders. At the

On the Pathless Pacific

stern a group of departing missionaries are singing hymns with their friends while a group of Chinamen at the bow exchange pleasantries with their countrymen on the dock. When the last gang plank is pulled off, we glide out into the bay followed by a shower of bits of yellow paper that float like butterflies in the air. They are the Chinese prayers for a good voyage and, to a person with a grain of superstition, they are a cheerful omen. I have turned my tortoise shell comb on my own country, and it is pleasant to have even Chinese good wishes for a safe return. So many possible perils lie before the stanchest ship as she follows her course across the lonely ocean. Today we are a thousand miles from anywhere and only one sail has been sighted, the faintest ghost of a sail far off on the horizon. Besides our own throbbing engines and the life that the ship bears with her, nothing suggests the existence of man. We leave behind us a broad path of foaming blue, but even before we lose sight of it in the distance the water has settled back into its old calm and forgotten us. Human life belongs to the soil. Old ocean fosters us only because ship builders have outwitted him. By the way, if any one desires to earn the title of "professional cheerupodist," let him spend his time writing steamer letters to his friends. Letters always gladden the heart of a wanderer from home and those received just as the homeland is fading away are perhaps the most grateful of all.

The City of Peking is no longer a frisky girl. She began her career some twenty-two years ago and now pursues her course as sedately as wind and weather permit. The sea has been very smooth, and few of the passengers have fallen victims to that most real and most unromantic of all afflictions—seasickness. Oh, the nothingness of nothing to do! The mild excitement of shuffle board and quoits wears itself out and walking the deck becomes a duty. One's head becomes a perfect sieve so far as catching ideas is concerned. Flying fish can't divert one for days at a time, and even the novel sight of seeing a pair of fine horses take a constitutional on the deck loses zest. The days are so nearly alike that I can't decide whether I got aboard yesterday or have been on forever. I have heard of a man who wasn't lazy, but a great lover of physical and mental calm. He must have liked the ocean. Yet it is a "sweet doing nothing"—*dolce far niente*—after all, and we have made many friends and shall see the City of Peking sail on for Hong-Kong without us with regret.

We have the usual gist of notables aboard. Baron Nissi, envoy extraordinary and minister plenipotentiary (!) of Japan to Russia, is returning, it is said, to take a position in the cabinet. He gained particular distinction for himself by his skillful management of Japanese affairs in Russia during the late war. The baron is a quiet, unassuming, courteous gentleman, hardly the man you would select as one who had hobnobbed with the czar of all the Russias. He is fond of whist and plays a good game.

Another interesting person is Mr. Frederick Yates, the English artist who has had many portraits in the

On the Pathless Pacific

Salon and Royal Academy. He talks most entertainingly of art and artists, indeed of anything, and furnishes much fun for the little folks with his song of the Royal Wild Beast Show. Mr. Yates' first commission when he returns to London will be the portrait of Sir Henry Irving. He has made several sketches of young ladies aboard and a notable one of Topsy, genial Captain Smith's favorite dog.

Topsy is a character. She is devoted to the captain but is not to be beguiled by soft blandishments from any one else and most often does not deign to turn her head when spoken to. Evidently Topsy has wearied of attention. When her majesty desires, however, she trots up to me, taps me on the knee, and when I take her up she tucks her nose in my sleeve and goes to sleep.

Lieutenant Autran of the Spanish navy and Lieutenant Mahan and Ensign Taylor, U. S. N., are going out to join their ships, and en route make most agreeable traveling companions. At the captain's table there are two round-the-worlders besides ourselves, Mr. Pettengill and Mr. Miller, of Cleveland, who stop, as we do, at the Hawaiian Islands to see Kilauea. We have, beside, jolly Mr. Main, English and entertaining, who says that when he puts his hat on his head it covers all his family.

Dinner table talk flits over topics grave and gay, wise and otherwise. Nobody could be dull within ten leagues of Captain Smith, for nobody spins a yarn better or laughs more heartily. It isn't unusual for me to run up against a bit of my own ignorance, something that everybody knows, with much the same feeling that one finds

One Way Round the World

a stone wall at the end of a lane, and I seem to have a rare field for it in nautical matters. One day the ball of conversation rolled to the subject of war ships and their immense weight. The discussion developed a question for your wise friend. He may know Archimedes' principle and how he discovered it, but again he may not. What is the principle of a ship's floating? Does an ironclad, for instance, weigh more or less than its displacement? It seems almost incredible to a person who knows nothing about it, that a heavy man-of-war displaces its weight of water, but the captain tells me that every vessel large or small displaces exactly its own weight, and that ship builders calculate to a nicety the weight of everything it is to carry, down to the instruments and crew, and construct the ship accordingly.

John Chinaman is a puzzle. They tell a story of a missionary who spent some months learning three or four hundred intricate Chinese characters and then when he got out to China he found he had learned them upside down. Chinese characteristics seem very much upside down too, as we study them, and yet we should have a care in passing judgment. I think people are apt to underestimate the intelligence of the Chinese, and the way initiated Americans are accustomed to speak of them and to them is a bit shocking to uninitiated ears. It is easy to fall into the error of thinking, because a person does something that seems to you foolish, that he necessarily is foolish. That the Chinaman—begging his pardon, for he prefers the correct word Chinese—does things in a different way from what we do, is too true, but that this is an evidence of his folly is not so easy to prove.

Once a Chinaman saw a young English woman playing a lively game of tennis and inquired how much she was paid for it. When he was told that she received nothing for the exertion he wouldn't believe it. It all depends on the point of view. Fortunately, though a somewhat conscientious sightseer, I don't feel under obligations to decide great questions one way or the other, so I still enjoy life a good deal.

Ah Sing and Ah Sang are a perennial feast of amusement for me. They are so different, yet so curiously alike, and the syllables play leap frog off the end of their tongues in such an entertaining way. One would think that after having twisted their tongues around Chinese, they could pronounce anything, but they speak English with a very marked accent.

Our steward is Ah Choo! The Wise One calls him Sneeze, because that is so much easier to remember. Ah Choo is a jewel. Even if he does speak English upside down, he is a faithful servant with a happy faculty for anticipating one's wants and remembering where he has seen things. Then there is little Ah You, thin as to frame and thin as to pig-tail, who always misunderstands before he understands you, and who works rapidly and incessantly from morning till night. Sometimes I see him squatting on the floor in the most uncomfortable attitude possible, washing the cups and saucers. He carefully tucks the end of his queue into his pocket to keep it out of his way. One day he came

One Way Round the World

along the deck with a cigarette between his lips. There was a booming breeze and I wondered how he was going to light it. What did he do but lift his wide sleeve, stick his head well into it and immerge a moment later with a glowing tip on the cigarette and a halo of smoke wreaths around his celestial pate.

Forward, we have a small Chinatown, where the Chinamen sit on the deck smoking and playing dominoes and chattering like magpies. Like the Indians, they have a superstition about being photographed, and skurry away when the camera appears.

The second day out we heard that a Chinaman in the steerage had died. He came on board in the last stages of consumption, and it seems he didn't expect to live to reach China for he had paid in San Francisco the $30 that the company charges for carrying a dead body into port. This is not at all unusual, for every Chinaman believes that unless he is buried in Chinese soil and his friends and family burn incense and say prayers over his grave he can not be happy in the future life. He expresses it something like this: "Suppose wantchee go topside, after kill, then wantchee family make chin-chin joss at grave. Suppose no take bones, no makee grave, no speakee chin-chin joss, then not belong topside at all after kill; belong hellee." So the steamship companies sign a contract when they take a Chinaman to America that they will bring him or his bones back to China.

One day I dropped into one of the long wicker steamer chairs for a chat with the ship's surgeon. When

On the Pathless Pacific

a man dies on board, the body is embalmed by the surgeon, put in a coffin and hoisted into one of the life boats. Part of the $30 goes to the surgeon and the Chinamen understand that he has something to gain by their death, so they are very distrustful of him and refuse to take any of his medicine. "Once," he said, "I offered a man who was dangerously ill some brandy and ginger. He refused to take it, saying there was poison in it. To convince him, I drank the glass myself and offered to get more for him. He wouldn't take it, however, and died a couple of hours later."

The Chinese have very peculiar methods of treating the sick. Sometimes they pinch the skin and pull it out as far as possible from the body, or sometimes they run needles in the flesh. Again, they put red powder that looks like brick dust in the nostrils. This heroic treatment, the surgeon says, often exhausts a sick man, and he dies very soon after it.

Moon waits on the captain's table. I believe he spells it Mun, but Moon suits him better. Moon wears a long white gown and looks as if he had just been washed and ironed. He slides noiselessly around on his felt-soled shoes; dignified, alert, watchful, indispensable.

. . . .

Last night we reached Honolulu. A glorious moon shone between the fleecy clouds and turned the sea to molten silver. It was past midnight but many of the passengers were on deck to catch that first, familiar, grateful glimpse of land. The lights of Honolulu

One Way Round the World

seemed to twinkle a welcome to us, as we sped along sending flaming rockets high into the air as a signal to the pilot to come and steer us safely through the coral reefs. The pilot once aboard, we were soon along side the dock, safely landed in the "Paradise of the Pacific."

FIRST GLIMPSE OF THE "PARADISE OF THE PACIFIC".

III

The Islands of the Pacific

WHEREVER the wind of fortune blows people of many nationalities together there arises a mass of incongruities. It is so in Honolulu. If one selects a half-dozen street corners in the city, they may suggest a half-dozen different countries, for people and colonies of all nations are there. The races, too, are very much intermingled, and it would take an expert mathematician to calculate the fractions of blood sometimes represented in one person. A dark-skinned fellow, darker than the native Hawaiian, was pointed out to me and I was told that his grandmother on one side was an East Indian and his grandfather a Chinaman. His father was a white man and yet he himself was almost as dark as a negro. The intelligence of these half breeds is considerably above the average and this particular man is extremely intelligent. He was educated at one of our colleges in the States. The pure-blooded Hawaiians are a handsome race, but the most regular features and finest physiques come from a mixture of the Hawaiian with white blood.

Incongruities of race go hand in hand with incongruities of dress. The "Mother Hubbard law" has not yet been passed in the Islands, it is evident, for the native

One Way Round the World

costume is a loose, full garment that is best described by that name. It is worn on all occasions, sometimes being made of silk and satin. If I remember my Mother Goose, Mother Hubbard was an attenuated little old lady who wore her original garment rather gracefully, but it is far from becoming to some of these Hawaiian belles, of truly amazing proportions. The original costume of the Islands was principally smiles and complexion and the ungainly loose gown was first introduced by the missionaries. It is said that the introduction of clothes has been fatal to the native race, for they are utterly careless about precautions against dampness and care in ventilation.

Another curious sight is a Chinaman in overalls or a Jap in a washpan hat and russet shoes. The sailor hat is a favorite, too, and is usually decorated with a wreath of natural flowers. Several times I've seen women who were barefoot, wearing a calico Mother Hubbard and a rather modish walking hat, adorned with flowers.

The language is very musical, easy to learn to understand, but difficult to learn to speak, for the native ear is quick to mark the slightest distinction in vowel sounds that we have difficulty in hearing. As there are twelve islands in the group so there are twelve letters in the alphabet, A-E-I-O-U-H-K-L-M-N-P-W, and every syllable and every word ends in a vowel. It is a curious fact that the natives of the Hawaiian Islands and the New Zealanders readily understand one another, though separated by five thousand miles of water. This is a sign that I copied from a building opposite the Arling-

The Islands of the Pacific

ton. It is a prosaic advertisement of lumber instead of a family romance, as one might imagine:

    Lui Ma
   Pa Kuai Papa
A Me Na Lako Kukulu Hale E A E
   A Na Amo Apau.

As to climate: It was Disraeli who said that to be young and to be in love and to be in Paris is to reach the height of human felicity, but he might have said Hawaii, for it seems a place cut out for lovers and honeymoons and beatific states in general. One has spirits to give away. The breeze is always so balmy, the sky so often blue, the climate so mild, that the Hawaiian language has no word to express the general idea of the weather. I don't know as yet with what they fill up gaps in conversation.

In Honolulu the gardens are a blaze of gorgeous color, relieved by lovely palms and *lacy*-foliaged trees that have the fresh green color of our early springtime. The vegetation is tropical and the lovely road to Waikiki, skirting the sea, runs through fields of banana plants and thick groves of tall cocoanut palms, many of them from fifty to seventy feet high. At this season the slender trunks are bent with the weight of the fruit. Only small boys dare to climb them, for the weight of a man at so great a height might snap the trunks. Our garden at the Arlington was full of clear-voiced birds and there was a magpie that whistled sweetly "Way Down Upon the Swanee River." An invalid who had spent many hours on the wide veranda had taught him, and as soon as he heard someone whistle the opening bar he would take up the strain and finish it. The Hawaiians are very musical and play and sing delightfully their simple tuneful airs. They use an instrument called an ukulele, a cunning diminutive guitar that I have already found irresistible and added to my possessions. The prettiest of the airs are sung to accompany the hula, a native dance. The ukulele is played with a peculiar strumming stroke, not unlike the banjo, and the same strain is repeated indefinitely until the dance is finished. There is something mournful about the monotonous minor strains that makes them seem appropriate national airs, for there is a pathos in the situation of these handsome, strong-limbed, dark-eyed islanders. The race seems destined to disappear and the government is already in the hands of outsiders and the monarchy hopelessly overthrown. There was no doubt a necessity for it, but a necessity to be regretted.

Liliuokalani is living in Honolulu at present and is occasionally seen driving in the streets. The young princess is a beautiful, finely-educated girl who has spent much of her life in England.

The "Kinau" plies between Honolulu and Hilo, where the ascent to the volcano of Kilauea begins, a journey of about thirty-six hours. She is a stanch little vessel with an amazing talent for standing on her nose, floundering on her side, or pirouetting on her stern with little or no provocation in the way of a rough sea. It is hard to collect one's thoughts at an angle of forty-five

THE GARDEN OF THE ARLINGTON, HONOLULU

The Islands of the Pacific

degrees, but there are many interesting things to write about.

The Kinau was due to sail at ten o'clock in the morning, but we didn't get away till noon and on the way outward waved good-bye to the City of Peking which was still in port. The dock was crowded with a truly miscellaneous crowd, and I was particularly interested in the native women who were selling long strings of blossoms of all colors, ingeniously fashioned into ropes and necklaces and hat-bands. I bought a beautiful red carnation "boa," and readily paid twenty-five cents for it, though I found afterwards that I might have had it for five. These strings of gay-colored flowers and garlands of leaves are a pretty Hawaiian fashion of saying good-bye, and some of the passengers were decorated with rope after rope of them.

I am indebted to Mr. Sam Parker for some brilliant fragrant strings that came on board for him at Hakone. They were arranged in bouquets that looked at first like huge cabbages, but when a string was cut the leaves fell back and the ropes of blossoms were ready to be unwound from the center. Anyone who has read Mitchell's clever story, "Amos Judd," will remember Molly Cabot's amazement, when, after having woven all sorts of romantic conjectures around the dark-skinned, foreign-looking man who stood near her, she inquired his name and was told that he was a Connecticut farmer and his name was Amos Judd. So Sam Parker is an ordinary and very American name to belong to the dark-skinned, magnificently built man who bears it. His grandfather, I believe, was a white man, but the rest of his ancestors were Hawaiian. He himself is the largest landowner in the islands, and has a beautiful home on the island of Hawaii, where the latchstring is ever out to his friends.

It is to Mr. Parker, also, that I am indebted for my first taste of poi, pronounced poy. Poi is a peculiar, gray, pasty substance made from the taro plant and is a food much liked by the natives. It has a sour, yeasty, not unpleasant taste and is very wholesome. Poi was not on the Kinau bill of fare but Mr. Parker and a number of the passengers had brought some with them. Mr. Parker said the last time he went to the States he took a barrel of it with him.

One's imagination is apt to lead one very far astray, but this trip among the islands is just as I had pictured it. They rise green and smiling from the ocean, sometimes in abrupt cliffs, sometimes in gently sloping fields. The island of Maui was particularly beautiful as we came to it at sunset. A lowering cloud hung over the crest of the mountain and threw out more strongly the brilliant color of the slopes. They were striped by barren bands that showed the warm red color of the soil, and it was explained to me that the trade winds blow with such regularity that they carry the moisture always in the same direction. If a peak projects that cuts off the moisture there is a barren strip across the land.

It was just at dusk that we saw a sight distressing to a lover of horses. The shores of most of the islands

The Islands of the Pacific

will not permit so large a vessel as the Kinau to come up to a dock, and all the landing is done in small boats. As it grew dark, I was leaning against the rail watching the boats that had put out from the Kinau coming back with the passengers. Two or three times I was puzzled by a peculiar snorting sound that seemed to come from that direction and finally, looking closely, I saw a horse's head alongside the boat. A man at the prow was holding his head out of the water with a strap, and the poor beast was struggling along, swimming as best he could and snorting painfully as he swallowed gulps of salt water. When the boat came alongside, the man at the prow swung the horse around between the small boat and the Kinau's side. The sea was rough and he seemed in imminent danger of being crushed between the boats. All the time the tedious and awkward work of getting him in a sling to swing him on board was being done, he choked and sputtered and swam frantically. He was hauled on board, too, with small courtesy and landed sprawling on the deck, quivering with fright. There were three horses put on in the same way and one of them came near drowning. It is the only way to carry them from one island to another, so it has to be done, but the swim is a long one and they are occasionally drowned, so frequently that the steamship company will not take any responsibility in the matter. Cattle are put on the same way, but pigs are brought out in the boats. A little later I heard a pig squealing lustily and looked down in time to see a portly porker picked up by four sailors and tossed on board.

Two or three times during the night I was awakened by those same ear-splitting, protesting yowls. Between times the anchor bumped up and bumped down again. An anchor is no doubt a very good thing at times but its method of getting itself up and down isn't the best of music to sleep by. In fact, all the comforts of home are not guaranteed on board the Kinau. It is said that her officers never admit she is rolling much unless the mast head dips up some sea moss. The chef was the high light in this truly Rembrandtish picture, for he gave us so many good things to eat. We tried a new kind of fruit that looks like a very much overgrown cranberry and tastes like rain-water.

. . . .

While I was sitting on deck, trying to stick to something solid, I made the beginning of my acquaintance with the Gonzales family. A dark-eyed, olive-skinned little boy was sitting on a bench opposite me, looking rather lonesome and a bit seasick. He had an attractive, handsome little face and before long we began a conversation. The child had been all over the islands, I discovered, and could talk intelligently and entertainingly of every one of them.

"I was born in Australia," he began, "and my father is a Chileno—that means born in Chili—but I'm an American. I like the United States best. My name is Carlos Gonzales." Then he went on to tell me that he had lived in Australia and in the States and in South

The Islands of the Pacific

America and in Europe, almost everywhere it seemed. He had nine brothers and sisters, he said, but all were dead except two sisters and himself. "My mother isn't a bit old yet," he explained. "She was married when she was thirteen. One of my aunts is a grandmother at twenty-seven! She was a mother at thirteen and her daughter was a mother at fourteen."

Those are his words just as he chose them and I noticed he referred very often to his own mother and seemed very fond of her. Several times he spoke of things that he did not do because she did not think them nice. I thought to myself, as I listened, that the mother must be a very lovely woman to have such a well-bred, manly little son. He was taking care of himself because she was very seasick, and after a while he felt so badly himself that he curled up and took a nap with his head on my knee. When he awoke he thanked me very gravely and politely and went away to see his mother. The ice was broken then and a little later we talked a long time together while I grew more and more charmed with the little fellow's character. You can imagine my surprise when I discovered that his father is the manager of a variety show that is traveling in the islands and that Carlos himself is one of the performers.

The father is an interesting man who has been in every known, and many, to me, unknown, parts of the globe. He seemed very fond of Carlos and pleased at the fancy I had taken to him. Once he turned to him and pinched his cheek lovingly. "He's a fine little fellow, if I do say it myself," he said. "He'll tell you something about every place he's been. When I came out this time I was going to leave him in school, where he'd ought to be, but when I told him, the look in his brown eyes just cut me to the heart and I had to bring him along."

Besides **Carlos,** there were two daughters, both very much like the boy, and with the same pretty manners. The stamp of the struggle for existence was plain upon all of them, the stamp of hard times and the rough life of second-rate variety show people, and I found myself wondering by what miracle they had kept a delicacy that was quite apparent and a lovely affection for one another.

In the evening a group of passengers assembled on the forward deck and sat till well toward midnight, while Mr. Coney played the guitar and the natives sang some of their tuneful melodies. The Gonzales family were there, and Nina, a little tot of about seven, danced the hula for us. Her dancing was wonderful for a child, the expression of an innate love for music, and I shall long remember her swaying, graceful, wind-blown little figure.

In the morning before they left us Carlos and Nina posed for a picture, and Carlos handed me a program of their entertainment. It was one of the usual flaming posters announcing in startling headlines the appearance of the wonderful Gonzales family. I squeezed tight the little brown hand that the little man extended to me, promising to leave him a picture and an American flag pin at the hotel in Honolulu; the picture that he might have a likeness of himself and Nina, and the pin because he is such an enthusiastic little patriot.

It was just as they were leaving that I had my first and last glimpse of Mrs. Gonzales. She was a very badly dressed woman who looked sordid and uninteresting, the very person that one would instinctively avoid. But I remembered the sweet reflection of herself in the mind of the little boy and realized more keenly than I had ever done before that we may look for good in everyone, and that the fair flower of refinement sometimes blooms in the most alien soil.

. . . .

In one of the much thumbed magazines in the hotel parlor at Hilo, I ran across these verses. What an admirable expression of the elusive, invigorating charm of the sea!

A SEA SONG.

Away with care! Away with grief!
Hurrah for life! Hurrah, we're free!
Away with sorrow! Perish wrong!
Hurrah, hurrah! The sea! The sea!
  Yo ho, the waves are dashing,
  Yo ho, the billows crashing,
  Yo ho, the spray goes flashing
      Down the bay.

Hurrah! the gulls are winging,
O'er bows the waves are flinging
The cooling, pelting, stinging
      Salt sea spray.

One Way Round the World

Away with care!   Away with grief!
Hurrah for life!   Hurrah, we're free!
Away with sorrow!   Perish wrong!
Hurrah, hurrah!   The sea!   The sea!

.   .   .   .

The trip to Kilauea was in a way disappointing. A month ago the crater was very active, but now it is slumbering, though evidently preparing for another outbreak. At present the famous lake of fire seems to have "swallered itself," like the squidgicumsquees. There is left only a wonderful bed of cooled lava that stretches away for miles, and a stupendous hole in the ground that sends up a cloud of sullen smoke, and one must be content to omit glowing lava and burning cinders. The proximity of a volcano where steam is blowing out of fissures in the lava, and the ground is hot beneath one's feet, is calculated to make one feel a bit pious and not over critical. There is never any telling what part of the crater may cave in at any moment, and in many places a rag thrown down in a crack in the lava will ignite immediately. It is a three mile walk across the bed to the yawning hole, and one is rather relieved to land again on terra firma, at the Volcano House, at least more firma than the lava bed. They look for earthquakes in Hawaii as we do for April showers, and Hilo has had as many as eighteen in thirty minutes.

The road through the jungle from Hilo to the Volcano House, a distance of thirty miles, is up hill both ways apparently, from the time the lumbering stage takes to get over the ground. It is a charming drive,

ON THE LAVA BED

The Islands of the Pacific

however, with an endless feast of tropical forest, rank and luxuriant, filled with every kind of lacy fern and palm.

The country is sparsely settled, but it is just now beginning to be opened up and there are many coffee plantations being started. Most of the bushes are too young to bear, but some of them are already five or six feet high, and one can see the scarlet coffee berries among the shining leaves.

. . . . . .

October 7th, we are off on the Doric for Yokohama, and twelve days later we should see the snow capped peak of fair Fujiyama. The weather has been most amiable, and it could hardly have the heart to fail us on that day.

The Doric, by the way, brings the first mail from the States since that we brought with us on the Peking. One feels very far out of the world with no mail and no cable. This letter must wait ten days before it starts eastward.

IV

In Yokohama

HERE we are in real Japan, where the people are so novel and the sights so curious that the far-away western world seems as illusive as "flowers in the mirror and the bright moon in the water." Everything is so strange that the feeling that I am dreaming never deserts me. Sometimes I feel like glancing cautiously around to make sure that my godet skirt hasn't been changed by some Japanese fairy godmother into a silken kimono, and that my leather belt is still itself instead of a gay colored obi, and that the kinks haven't straightened out of my hair nor my eyes tilted up, and that I am still my American self instead of little Miss Moonshine or Miss Perfume or Miss Cherry Blossom.

You may take this for wild exaggeration but it is the solemn truth. Perhaps that wonderful waste of water that separates us from this land of queernesses is responsible. Sailing an apparently pathless ocean for twelve days gives a mind constructed like a sieve time to forget almost everything that has ever been poured into it. By day, a wide sea, reflecting nothing but clouds and the varying tints of the sky, by night, a waving, shining mirror that reflects the moon and stars and loneliness.

"MISS MOONSHINE, MISS PERFUME AND MISS CHERRY BLOSSOM."

In Yokohama

Not a sail, not a sign of life in all the long voyage from Honolulu to Yokohama.

We steamed into port at night and our first assurance that unfamiliar Japan lay just beyond us was a globe of light on the horizon, too steady to be a star and round and glowing enough to make one fancy it a big paper lantern hung from the corner of some dipper in the sky. It was really the first lighthouse of Nippon, as the Japanese call Japan, and before long, guided by its cheery beam, we were safe in the harbor of Yokohama with the thousand twinkling lights of the city in crescent shape around us. The passengers were not permitted to land that night, but apparently everything else was, to judge from the whack! bang! slam! crack! that cannonaded over our heads as we tried to sleep. In port the passenger finds his place of importance usurped by mail and cargo and is apt to wish he'd come over by a postage stamp himself.

Early in the morning I peered curiously through the port-hole that had framed so many seascapes for me and caught a glimpse of the low-lying green shores of Nippon. One green shore is apt to be much like another and I don't know that I should have recognized that one as foreign, but there, skimming along the water, was one of the square sailed little boats that I've seen sailing the main on so many paper fans. Without a doubt it was Japan.

A little later, from the deck we had a rare view of the beautiful harbor full of stately men-of-war and dozens of other smaller craft, with lofty snow-capped Fujiyama in the distance. It is related that a fat and infuriated tourist who attempted to ascend fair Fujiyama referred to it as a disgusting mass of humbug and ashes, but he probably thought better of his remarks when he reached sea level and caught his breath. Its cone-shaped slopes with their rim of glistening snow combine a singular grace and majesty and we counted it a good omen that the weather god slid back his screens of clouds and let us have our first view of the "honorable mountain" in clear sunshine. Everything is honorable over here, and you even ask the bell boy for honorable hot water, if your knowledge of the language permits the luxury of the Japanese form of speech. It may be, too, that the weather god does not arrange his weather effects on screens and slide them back and forth, but if he does not he fails to conform with approved Japanese methods.

There are so many strange things in this little land that a bewildered first-weeker doesn't know where to begin to tell about them. Like the old lady who lived in the shoe, I have so many impressions I don't know what to do. Sliding is one of them. Everything slides. The statement is a broad one and I might have to retract it in some instances, but that is a general impression. In the morning as you walk along the streets, the fronts of the houses are sliding open. Inside you can see rooms sliding open and shut and into one another in a most bewildering fashion, and I'm not sure that even whole houses do not accidentally slide together. This sounds so incredible that I shall have to explain promptly that Japanese houses are a flimsy combination of matting

JAPANESE JUNKS

In Yokohama

and screens, windowless and chimneyless, suggesting bird-cages more than dwellings for human beings. They have a wooden lattice in front, and the light is admitted through screens of tough white Japanese paper that is more or less immaculate according to the dignity of the establishment. When curious to know what is going on in the street or next door, the Japanese wets the side of his house with his tongue, sticks his finger through it and calmly gazes through the aperture. Glass is beginning to be used somewhat, small squares of it being set in the white paper screens, but it is still such a novelty that the car windows have a line of white paint across them, to show that there is something there, and thereby prevent the people from bumping their heads or breaking the glass. The people slide, too. They either go barefoot or wear a curious white stocking with a pocket for their big toes, and they always walk on either straw or wooden clogs. The clogs have a strap, and young and old are very expert at twisting their big toes around it and holding on, but they have to walk with a peculiar sliding gait that is ungainly and ungraceful. On the hard pavements of the railway stations there arises such a chorus of scrapes that the noise of the little narrow-gauge train must feel ashamed of itself.

I said everything slides, but I forgot the jinrikishas. You yourself are in some danger of sliding off the seat, but the jinrikisha itself has wheels, two of them. Everybody who has been to Japan has written about it, but, like love, the subject is ever new; probably no one has ever resisted describing the little vehicle and his first ride in one. As we emerged in Indian file from the clutches of the Custom House, we were confronted by a row of little men in toadstool hats and puckered pantaloons, who cried out persuasively, "Riksha? Riksha?" pointing to a curious combination of a baby carriage and a sulky that stood just behind them. We hadn't read up on Japan for nothing, so we hailed our men like veterans and clambered in. I found myself wondering whether we would next be presented with a rattle and rubber ring, but they picked up the shafts sedately and started down the Bund, a promenade along the sea wall, at a brisk run. My runner sped along so easily and his muscular legs looked so strong, that I forgot to feel sorry for him as I had expected, and enjoyed myself instead. We rode up with a flourish to the Grand Hotel, a famous hostelry where everybody goes in Yokohama, kept by an affable German, and very un-Japanese. The Wise One and I wish we had the courage of our convictions, and we would stop at Japanese inns and see more of the life of the people there; but no one who has not tried it knows how nearly impossible it is to give up one's habits of living and adapt one's self to a different order of things. Beds and chairs and tables are luxuries that we forget to be thankful for except when we haven't them, and my recollection of my first Japanese meal leaves me no desire for another course of mysteries.

.   .   .   .

Yokohama we found delightful. I wish we could keep the freshness of our interest with us always, but it

A JAPANESE LADY IN HER JINRIKISHA

In Yokohama

is sure to slip away. Like the etching there is nothing quite equal to the first, the artist's proof, and it is Yokohama that will remain clearest in memory.

We strolled up and down the narrow streets picking up curios that struck our fancy, never tiring of the quaint little open shops with their matting floors, big fire pots and vases of chrysanthemums. They are all decorated with blue strips of cloth covered with white characters which presumably tell the names of the firms and the character of the merchandise. These waving banners give a festive appearance to the street, and the silk shops have the most realistic side show effects. I never could get over the feeling that I had forgotten to pay the admission. The godowns are another curiosity, heavy fire-proof warehouses apparently so named because they are the only things that do not go down in the case of fire. The merchants store their best goods in these godowns, and carry them out into the shops when customers appear. The Benten-dori and the Honcho-dori are the principal shopping streets where you can buy everything Japanese, from delicate ivory carvings and rich embroideries to egg-shell porcelain and wondrous cloisonné.

One morning, as we were rikshaing to the Bentendori for a shopping jaunt, we passed a curious procession in the street. First came two or three dozen blue and white-coated Japs carrying enormously tall blue banners decorated with every conceivable nightmare of the alphabet in staring white. The usual crowd of small boys attended the advance guard—but such small boys!—

One Way Round the World

Animated posters every one of them, dressed in every color of the rainbow, clumping along with a tremendous clatter on their high wooden clogs. A funeral! thought I, for it much resembled a funeral procession that had been pointed out to me, at a distance, the day before. The position was admirable for a snap shot, for the group of banners was followed by a mysteriously ornamented wagon that was attracting the respectful attention of passersby. I pressed the button. A closer inspection revealed little that I had expected and much that I had not. The lower part of the wagon was so concealed with ornaments and hieroglyphics that the interior couldn't be seen, but a familiar device on the top sent a chill along my spine. It was a pasteboard imitation of a huge arm, brandishing a battle ax. Let us hope for the best, but to this day I am not sure whether that brilliant procession with its banners, its kaleidoscopic colors and its delicious small boys was a funeral procession or an advertisement of Battle Ax plug tobacco.

It is a matter of everlasting regret that I haven't a photograph as a clue. Japan is not a paradise for snap shots, and the camera manufacturers warn the amateurs against disaster. The sun rarely shines brightly enough for good results. It is particularly unfortunate, too, for though the Japanese understand the mechanical process of photography admirably they have little taste in the selection of subjects and no appreciation of the charm of naturalness. There are few photographs of street scenes to be found in the shops and almost none of children, while the background of the Japanese lady at home is apt to show the edges of the photographer's screens and the jinrikisha runner has a palpably manufactured Fujiyama rising conspicuously just over his left shoulder.

. . . .

"And so you have the great Ito for your guide," said an English woman to me at breakfast. "Really you are fortunate, unless his reputation gained through Miss Bird has spoiled him."

We made our acquaintance with Ito when he was shown up to our rooms at the Grand Hotel soon after our arrival—a most fascinating little figure, short even for a Jap, dressed in full Japanese silk costume, a harmony of soft grey-blues. He entered in a series of wonderful bows, so low that I'm sure he couldn't have lowered them a sixteenth of an inch more if I had been the Queen of England. When he finally came back to first position, he at once began to state the object of his call, in quaint, refined English, and when he had presented his card and credentials, explained his duties as a guide, and expressed a wish that he might accompany us, he bowed all the way out from the center of the room again and retired. We were so pleased with him that we could hardly wait for the time appointed next day when we should complete arrangements. The only trouble, we decided, would be to live up to Ito. An innate gentleness and polish seemed to belong in a superlative degree to the dear little man in flowing robes and sandaled feet, and on the question of bows we were bound to be distanced. What was our dismay when Ito appeared next day in the prosaic European costume, sadly commonplace in comparison with the day before, but still polite and prepossessing. We remonstrated with him for changing his clothes, but he explained that the European style of dress is much more convenient for traveling, and with a sigh we relinquished the ideal for the practical.

Of course, 'twould be more independent, or, at least more out of the ordinary, to travel without a guide; but when one's Japanese vocabulary is limited and one's appetite is good, an assistant is necessary. Already Ito has proved himself useful and agreeable, and has saved us a world of bother, to say nothing of his being a peripatetic guide book, a complete substitute for our red-backed Murray. Eighteen years ago, Ito was only a lad, but as servant and guide to Miss Isabella Bird, he was so efficient and faithful, so alert and intelligent in conducting her through "Unbeaten Tracks in Japan" that he won for himself the distinction of great praise in that charming book, and has ever since been constantly in demand as the most desirable of Japanese guides.

. . . .

We are spending the night in Tokyo, on our way to Nikko in the mountains. The autumn foliage is just now in full glory and we want to see it at its best.

. . . . . .

V

Japanese Customs and Beliefs

THERE is a Japanese proverb: "Nikko no mi nai uchi wa, 'Kekko' to ui na!" "Do not use the word magnificent till you have seen Nikko!" I didn't translate it myself but have it upon Ito's authority. You can not imagine the strange Babes-in-the-Wood sensation of being dependent on another person for every word that you wish to speak or understand. I have learned "Ohayo," pronounced "Ohio" which means good morning, and there, with the addition of "Ikura," how much, and "Sayonara," good-bye, my vocabulary rests for the present. It is true that I have learned to count quite glibly up to a hundred, but as I have never yet understood a number when attached to yen and sen, dollars and cents, they haven't been valuable. Japanese names of places seem to be as slippery as their favorite eels and it is only by a strenuous effort that the arrangement of the syllables is persuaded to stay by me. Tokyo and Kyoto, for instance, are the same syllables in different order, and there are many more intricate resemblances. The mere mention of some of our mistakes is a signal for hilarity. In Tokyo we called upon Mr. Montono, Secretary to the Minister of Foreign Affairs, to whom

One Way Round the World

we had a letter of introduction some two or three yards long. Before we left I narrowly escaped calling that august gentleman Mr. Kimono, a kimono being the long, loose outer garment that Japanese men and women wear. Ito mixes up with Nikko, Myanoshita is warranted unrememberable, and so on ad infinitum. I credit myself with the discovery that some of our American slang has come to us from Japan. Our expression "all hunky dory" might easily be a corruption of Honchodori, Yokohama's swagger business street, and when we call a man a great gun we are probably comparing him to the illustrious shoguns of this country. Chuzenji we remember by "choose N. G.," and that reminds me that it was Chuzenji and Nikko that I began to talk about.

The province of Nikko is famous for its temples and the glorious tints of its autumn foliage, and as the tints are just now in full brilliancy, we hurried north from Yokohama, stopping only a day in Tokyo, that we might see them at their best. Truly one would have to reserve magnificent and a good many superlative adjectives beside, to describe them. Yesterday we went to Chuzenji, a day's ride in jinrikishas, and for miles along these beautiful valleys the mountains are one blaze of gorgeous color. I don't think that Jack Frost dips his brush in his paint box any more lavishly than in our own Indiana, but we haven't the mountain slopes to unfurl his banners on. It was an enchanting day, a perfect riot of color and sunshine. When we rode in under the trees the branches laced themselves above

TEMPLE ENTRANCE AT NIKKO

Japanese Customs and Beliefs

our heads like a gay-hued parasol, and when we came suddenly upon a long vista, as we did many times, we could see the mountains in carnival array for miles, dotted with foaming, splashing mountain torrents.

The road is a steep, rocky, mountain path, badly washed by the late disastrous floods, and it remains a marvel to me how my runners ever got me up and down it alive. There were three of them to each jinrikisha and they pushed me up places that I could scarcely have dragged myself alone. They tug and strain and pull uncomplainingly, singing a monotonous, meaningless chant, and of course they are muscular and hardened to it, but one has only to look at them, dripping with perspiration and panting for breath when they stop for a short rest, to see that they do desperately hard work. The poor fellows have only rice to eat, which isn't sustaining enough for such violent exertion, and they rarely live to be more than forty years old, usually dying of heart disease. Occasionally my sympathy would be too great and I'd get out and walk, but the climb was so fatiguing that I'd soon have to get in again. These coolies are only paid forty cents, gold, a day, but you may be sure we sent them on their way rejoicing with a liberal fee.

We lunched at Chuzenji, on the bank of a lovely lake that is hemmed in on all sides by the same frost-frescoed mountains which reflect their colors in metallic glints in the clear water. After lunch we visited another of the innumerable temples of the district, and saw the sacred mountain, the Mecca of Japanese pilgrims, with its grand old head in a silvery cloud. The ride up had been rough enough but the ride down was worse. Every step of the coolies meant a more or less vicious jolt for me, and last night as I rubbed my aching muscles, I didn't know which I felt sorriest for, my worn out runners or myself! Yet somebody dared to call jinrikisha riding the poetry of locomotion! How fortunate it is that the beauties and pleasures of traveling remain in the memory and the discomforts are so easily forgotten. I shall remember the day as enchanting, a little journey into fairyland, and the weariness is already gone.

It is our good fortune to be in Nikko for a special festival, and we have seen a number of the royal princes and princesses. This morning we saw a procession go over the sacred bridge of red lacquer over which only royalty is allowed to pass. I noticed that the coolies who were carrying the palanquins as well as other attendants were allowed to pass over the bridge, and I asked Ito if they did not consider it a great honor to have crossed it. He shrugged his shoulders. "They do not care," he said. "Why should they? We, in Japan, do not care for things that are not for us. If this or that is for the gods, well, let it be so. It is only Americans who wish much to do what they must not." I accepted the estimate of my countrymen meekly for I had been thinking, not three minutes before, that I should like to go across the bridge. "Why?" as Ito said.

They are having the celebration here—celebration is

Japanese Customs and Beliefs

hardly the word, for it is more like a funeral to the Japanese—because they are bringing back the teeth and Buddha bone (Adam's apple) of two of the royal princes, who died in Formosa during the war, to deposit them in a temple here among the mausoleums of the shoguns. The processions have been circuses for for us, however. Such costumes, such people, such music! Pitti Sings and Kokos and Peep Boos in real life, even a shade more whimsical than they were in the tuneful "Mikado." Indeed, I think I should have to live here a long time before I could realize that these active little people are anything more than large editions of the Japanese dolls with which we are familiar. The children are exact fac-similes of them. The women are not so beautiful nor even so pretty as many hysterical books on Japan would lead one to believe, but they are cunning and charming. Their hair is a marvel. It is greased to make it as black and as straight as possible, and then it is arranged in elaborate puffs and coils, a style that seems particularly suited to Japanese features. Oddly enough, the little women are prettiest when they are rouged and powdered. The rice powder gives a creamy *matte* appearance to their smooth skins, and a touch of carmine accentuates the curves of their pretty lips. Just underneath the lower lip they often have a flake of gold leaf. Perhaps it is because there is no pretense at naturalness, that the rouge is not offensive as with us. They are frankly painted and it suits them.

The grown-up princesses in the procession were dressed

in European toilettes fresh from Paris and sadly unbecoming to them, but the little girls wore rich costumes of flowered crepe and their satiny hair was arranged in marvelous wheels. Their skins were smoothly powdered and their lips brightly tinted, and altogether they were as dainty little maidens as one could wish to see. I'm afraid though, that with those wheels and loops and puffs of hair to take care of, they don't have as good times as our own little girls.

The last of the deposed shoguns is still living, and his son, who is now a member of parliament, was one of the party—a stout, uninteresting individual in badly fitting European clothes. It is to be hoped that the reaction against European dress will continue to react and that the Japanese will not persist in wearing a costume in which they are so insignificant, instead of their own graceful style.

The temples of Nikko describe themselves better in photographs than I could hope to describe them in words. In architecture they are like nothing I have seen, wonderfully elaborate and yet stamped with a certain sobriety that is noticeable in Japanese taste, which makes their decorations elegant instead of gaudy. The interiors of the temples are one mass of lacquer and color and gold so skillfully combined and relieved that the effect is perfect.

The difference in architecture enables one to distinguish the Shinto from the Buddhist temples, but to distinguish the religion is another pair of sleeves, as the French say. Shintoism and Buddhism once became so

JAPANESE GIRLS

Japanese Customs and Beliefs

badly mixed up in Japan that it took an emperor's edict to "purify" and separate them. Now the Shinto temples are severely plain, with only a round mirror and strips of white paper at the altar, emblems of self-examination and purity of life. The reputed divine ancestress of the Mikado, Ten Sho Dai Jin (great goddess of the celestial effulgence!) is the chief deity. Three commandments were issued in 1872 as a basis of this made-over Shinto and national religion.

1. Thou shalt honor the gods and love thy country.
2. Thou shalt clearly understand the principles of heaven and the duty of man.
3. Thou shalt revere the emperor as thy sovereign and obey the will of his court.

Whether these mixed up people ever untangled their beliefs I do not know, but I suspect that they did not, for in spite of the purification, Buddhism remains the more powerful religion. The Buddhist temples are very ornate and contain much beautiful work in metals and carved wood. The images of Buddha are guarded by a stork and lotus, and often the image is seated on a lotus flower. As the exquisitely pure and fragrant lotus grows out of the mud of the pond, so, they think, the human mind should rise above earthly conditions into the pure region of spiritual life. Theirs seems to be a beautiful religion in theory but not in practice, and many of their texts are so profound that they make me laugh. Here's one of them: "Naught is everywhere and always, and is full of illusion." Who would not

One Way Round the World

long for a dreamless Nirvana if given much of that kind of spiritual food?

Of course we went to the tomb of Ieyasu, in Nikko, a climb of 7,631 steps—that is, I didn't count them, but I'm sure there were no fewer. All of these temples are at the tip top of a steep hill, and unless one's religious convictions are unusually strong, one is apt to grumble a good deal before the last one is crossed off the list. Ieyasu was a much revered shogun warrior, the Napoleon of Japan, whose spirit is still thought to roam over the earth, I believe, for a sacred horse is kept in a sacred stable in the temple yard, so that he may have it handy when he needs it. We bought the sacred horse some sacred beans which he gobbled up as unceremoniously as any unsanctified horse would have done, and nickered for more. Three carved monkeys on a panel of this sacred stable illustrate a Japanese maxim. One holds his ears, another covers his eyes and the third holds his hands over his lips, for the proverb runs, "Hear not too much, see not too much, speak not too much." Just in front of the stable there is a tall tree which Ieyasu is said to have carried around in a flower pot when he was on earth. On the opposite side of the court we threw an offering to a weird little priestess in flowing white garments who rose wearily and danced a sacred dance, gracefully waving a fan and some tinkling bells—not to amuse or edify us, if you please, but the spirit of the departed Ieyasu.

And the trees. If I haven't told you of the evergreens till now, it is not that I have forgotten them. Would

THE MONKEYS AT NIKKO

Japanese Customs and Beliefs

that I could put a window in my letter and let you see for yourselves the regal groves of lofty cryptomerias that cluster round the temples and rise majestically beyond them in slopes of dark, rich green. There is a stateliness and beauty about them that is indescribable, and in sunshine or in shade they are one long feast of loveliness to the eyes. The groves could spare the temples, but the temples could illy spare the groves. The climate of Nikko is even more tearful than that of the rest of Japan, and all growing things spring up in rank luxuriance. Everything is beautifully green. A hundred feathery mosses cling to the damp walls, and embroider fanciful designs on the carved stone lanterns. It is a wonderfully effective setting for this rare handiwork of man, a glory of art and nature that is a sermon.

VI

Tokyo and Elsewhere

WHILE I am waiting for a half-past seven dinner that is a good hour behind my appetite, I'll chat with my Indiana friends and enliven the delay. It is too bad that writing when one is traveling can not always be done when one is fresh, and before a sharp impression on the retina of the mind has been dimmed by another and still another. My inspirations are never over lustrous, but I trust this is one of those comfortable correspondences where my readers will sift out the ideas, if there are any, and pardon the slip when there are none, so that I may go zigzagging from one topic to another with as little regard for order as Japanese fields have when they go zigzagging over the landscape.

We came away from lovely Nikko, leaving several waterfalls unvisited. We might have entertained ourselves there indefinitely, visiting the beautiful glens of the neighborhood, but, as the Wise One says, the water falls in Japan much the same as it does in America, and it is the people we want to see. We reveled again in the toy railway that runs from Nikko to Tokyo, and made merry over the teacups. Tea! Tea! Tea! I'm sure we have drank enough to float a ship already.

Tokyo and Elsewhere

When you enter your compartment in the train, you find the inevitable tea table with a kettle of boiling water and a supply of tea ready to be served to the passengers. The Japanese decoction tastes more like stewed grass than anything else and is served without milk or sugar, so we sugar lovers have to draw on our supply of bonbons to sweeten it. Every time I taste it, I vow that I'll never be led into that same indiscretion again, but the next time I am sure to be beguiled by the one-armed little teapot and the little handleless cups and the smiling little handmaiden who offers it, and take another dose. You see that the word "little" is apt to be very much overworked in telling of Japan. Everything is diminutive, almost nothing grand or great. You seem to be looking at the place through the wrong end of an opera glass. It has all the charm of a miniature.

The territory between Nikko and Yokohama is one great garden, stretching away in unfamiliar, irregular fields of rice and taro and lotus, with occasional clumps of tea bushes and groves of fantastic pines and feathery bamboo; all cultivated by hand with primitive agricultural implements. Men and women work in the fields, bareheaded and barefooted always, some of them coming perilously near being barefooted all over. One only needs to travel to learn that the term propriety is entirely relative. You must readjust your opera glasses on that subject, too. We are here in the cold season, when the most clothing is worn, yet we see men working in the blacksmith shops in the open street in the costume of Adam before the fall, and men and women

One Way Round the World

bathing unconcernedly scarcely six feet away from the passersby. They see absolutely no impropriety in that, yet are wonderfully shocked at some customs introduced by Europeans, dancing, for instance. It is a queer world, is it not?

Even in this cold weather, when we are wearing our warmest clothing, our coolies sometimes wear only a thin cotton jacket. I have seen them shaking with cold before starting, but they are soon perspiring in streams when they get to work. Another time I shall tell you about what these and other laborers are paid. Just a few things more about the country and we'll arrive at Tokyo.

The country houses are picturesque little buildings with wonderfully heavy thatched roofs, often two feet thick, that sometimes have a festive little garden growing along the ridge. They have the same paper screens and clean mats, even though the whole family and the farm animals as well are living under the same roof. No wonder one is in danger of being bamboozled in a country where bamboo is used for everything; furniture, water pipes, fences, buckets, weather boarding, laths, canes, baskets, umbrella ribs, lanterns, twine, roofing, nails—and now I've just begun! When it is young the shoots are eaten as we eat asparagus, and the tough fullgrown poles are turned into everything from delicate carving to the heavy supports of dwellings. The rice fields are very curious to us, too. Rice will only grow in water, so the fields have to lie in the lowlands where they can be flooded and the workers stand up to

Tokyo and Elsewhere

their knees in slimy mud. It is first sown in seed and then transplanted to the water fields, a tedious, weary process. When the shoots are young and low the water is plainly seen, but when the grain is ready for cutting it has grown tall and thick, and does not look unlike our wheat fields at home.

. . . .

Never in my life have I been in a place where one's slightest wants presented such enormous difficulties and where there is such a superb indifference to the flight of time. Yokohama seemed strange to us at first, but I regard it as the acme of civilization since I have been to Tokyo. For one thing, we were very unfortunate about our guide. Our treasure, Ito, was taken very ill when we had barely gotten through congratulating ourselves on having him, and had to go to a hospital in Tokyo, leaving us to the tender mercies of Matsu. Matsu meant well, I think, but it was utterly impossible either to get anything into his head or out of it and we exchanged him as politely and as soon as possible for Suzuki, who is delightful, bright and willing, speaking English very well, and we pray nothing will prevent his accompanying us as far as Nagasaki, where we sail for Shanghai.

Matsu was with us all the time we were in Tokyo, and oh, what circuses we had in that never-ending, bewildering city, trying to find out where we were going and what we were seeing. Once we were uncertain whether we had arrived at the houses of parliament or a wall paper factory. If I lived there forever I should not try to get that maze of a map in my mind. I shouldn't have room for anything else. Imagine a one-storied city of a million and a half souls, plentifully interspersed with gardens and parks, moats within moats and even wide fields that suggest the open country, and think what magnificent distances it could afford. The streets are wide and laid out like a spider web, and the "man power carriage" (literal translation of jinrikisha) is the only way of riding, so you may count on one, two, three hours traveling from the time you leave your hotel till you get to the place you are going to visit. Nothing about Tokyo suggests a city except the tramcars in the main street, into which you wouldn't venture. It is always through a quaint, never-ending village that you seem to be going, with the same little shops and unreadable signs and strange little people clumping along on their clogs or standing in groups smilingly chattering a queer unknown tongue until they catch sight of yourself, and then they all stop what they are doing, even the babies, and stare at the wonderful spectacle that you yourself present. It never ceases to amuse me that I am much more of a curiosity to them than they are to me. One afternoon we went out to Asakusa, a big public park, where we were followed around all the time by at least two hundred round-eyed, astonished Japs, who stared at me in frank, childish amazement, and evidently commented wonderingly on my clothes. If I stopped for a moment, they crowded around so close that I could hardly move on again. One little girl looked at me earnestly for several minutes and then ran away as fast as she could. In a minute she returned leading a still smaller child by the hand and showed me to him, with explanations. Some of the children were afraid and scampered away as fast as they could if I turned in their direction. Everywhere the mothers ran to get their children to see us and sometimes the babies screamed with fright. Paterfamilias does not attract so much attention, for a few Japanese men wear European clothes, and many of them are already wearing grotesque passé derby hats and every conceivable monstrosity in the way of caps. But the hats and dresses of the Wise One and myself are a wonderful sight for them. Some jeweled trimming on an old velvet cape of mine which, by the way, hails from Indianapolis, seems to please them immensely and they often walk up, eye it admiringly, and rub it gently and turn it over chattering among themselves. I imagine they think they are real jewels and take me for at least a rajah's daughter. In the tea houses they ask me, through our interpreter, how much it cost, and invariably give vent to round oh's of astonishment when I tell them the rather modest sum I paid for it. I am told that the Japanese mean it as a compliment when they ask you what a thing costs or what your income is, for that shows a personal interest in your affairs. It is pleasant to be in a land where one's old clothes are so appreciated.

It seems to me that nowhere is there so much importance attached to dress as in America, and in the cramped space allotted me for logic, I have been trying to find a reason for it. In Europe and here in the

One Way Round the World

Orient so many charming and refined people, travelers from all lands of the globe, are, according to our standards, badly dressed—in materials and making inferior to what our middle class consider necessary for their position. Their attitude might be described as indifferent. I have opined, that in America, though we admit it reluctantly, where we have no aristocracy, the standard of position is largely that of money, and so there is a greater effort made to dress elegantly than in parts of the world where classes are more clearly defined. The Japanese give us an example in their lack of ostentation, freedom from the capricious rule of fashion, and simplicity of housekeeping and social life. However, though I observe and deduce, I'm true to American traditions. The trouble is that I shall have a gaping hole where a pocketbook ought to be when I get back to Paris and furbelows, if I continue to be beguiled by these tempting things in the Orient. Japan is bad enough and China, Siam, Ceylon and India are yet to be weathered. Everything is incredibly cheap. The Japanese do not know how to work badly. "The gods see inside," says the workman as he carefully finishes his piece of pottery or lacquer work, and as labor is so pitifully cheap, you can buy a thousand of their dainty fashionings, perfect in design and workmanship, for a few sen in the shops. Even the guide book says: "Any one who has money in his purse should not fail to visit the fascinating shops of Kyoto." In Yokohama I bought a wadded red silk crêpe dressing sacque lined with silk and beautifully and elaborately embroid-

AN APPROVED JAPANESE MACKINTOSH

ered with chrysanthemums for three dollars, gold. That is only an instance of the prices. Probably if I had been a more clever bargainer I might have had the dressing sacque for two dollars and fifty cents. These merchants sell for what they can get. They gauge your desire for the article to a nicety. As Sarah Jeannette Duncan says, "They anticipate your ideas even when you haven't any." Then you must do a deal of polite haggling if you wish to get the article at anywhere near a reasonable price, that is, a reasonable profit for the merchant, and no matter what you finally pay you are uncomfortably sure that the beady-eyed little heathen has got the better of you.

．　　．　　．　　．　　．　　．　　．　　．　　．

We saw Tokyo in all its moods while we were there. In bright sunshine, when it was gay and cheery, then gray and slashed with rain drops, with the pebbly streets a sea of mud and full of big oiled paper umbrellas held closely over shuffling figures in gray kimonos and high clogs suggesting a lot of toadstools out on a lark. Occasionally, we would pass a little man who looked as if he had jumped into a haystack by mistake, but he was only wearing an approved Japanese mackintosh made of rice straw.

We did our duty as conscientious sight-seers, visiting the chrysanthemum show, Ueno Park, the Shiba temples and bazaar, the government printing office, the arsenal gardens and all the rest. The chrysanthemum show was a grievous disappointment to all of us. We had expected specimens of rare and beautiful blossoms, but had to content ourselves with curious figures formed of the growing plants twisted into shape; ingenious, certainly, but stiff and ugly. There were scenes from the theater, many gruesome ones of executions, tea houses with geisha dancers, waterfalls, tidal waves and earthquakes, all fashioned of blossoms after the people's own peculiar ideas. The figure I liked best was a likeness of Japan's famous actor, Dan-juro. The show was not in a big building but in a lot of little booths, along a hilly street, into which two cents admittance was paid. The figures were arranged on circular platforms that slowly revolved, giving two separate scenes for your investment.

As at Asakasu, we found ourselves the center of attraction, more of a show than the chrysanthemums.

And just here let me set down our undying gratitude to dear, lively Mrs. Nishigawa, our table companion on the Doric, and our good friend, who so kindly steered us through the shoals of royal etiquette and made our stay in Tokyo doubly pleasant. Mrs. Nishigawa is an Englishwoman who married a Japanese and has lived for years in Tokyo, where she has a charming little English home in the heart of Japandom, and where we met her interesting family. She knows everyone and has evidently captivated everyone as she did us by her wit and grace. It was she who taught her Majesty the Empress, English, so she knows all about the royal family, and is well acquainted with all the chamberlains and equerries and what not dignitaries that mix themselves up in my democratic mind.

FUJI IN CHRYSANTHEMUMS

VII

The Mikado's Birthday

IT was due to Mrs. Nishigawa that we had tickets for the legation tent for the review on the emperor's birthday. This was November third. Early in the morning we were off from the hotel. It had threatened rain the night before but the morning came clear, frosty and cloudless. The streets were gay with flags, a big red disc on a white ground, and as we drew near the parade ground we were jostled by a lively, bustling, holiday crowd, all eager for a glimpse of the Mikado. Finally we came out on the great open field, where infantry and artillery and cavalry were already grouping themselves for the review, and scurried across to the tent next to the one decorated with the conventional chrysanthemum, which was reserved for the emperor. While we were awaiting his arrival we had plenty to divert us. Never have I seen so much brilliancy in the way of medals and gold lace and embroidery. As we sat there the military and naval attachés of the different legations appeared in resplendent uniforms, then the ministers and their suites in court costumes, then many Japanese officers and generals. The Corean minister and his suite wore curious costumes of blue and green changeable silk adorned with a square set just between the shoulders, embroidered with storks. On their heads they wore a device that looked more like a fly trap than anything else American, and around their waists they had a wondrous jeweled belt that was about the diameter of a barrel hoop. The Chinese minister came along as I was standing beside Mrs. Nishigawa and stopped to pay his respects. He had a beautiful robe of rich brocaded silk and a little black cap with a red knob, and as he walked away Mrs. Nishigawa murmured, "Do you know I never can help wishing for one of those robes for a drapery." The rest of the representatives wore uniforms of one sort or another. I most admired the naval attaché of the Spanish legation, a beautiful combination of red and blue and black embroidered with silver fleur-de-lis, and crowned with a jaunty hat of black and silver on which there trembled a bunch of snow white cock's plumes. Pardon me for speaking of the attaché as if he were only a uniform, a clothes horse, as Carlyle says, on which clothes are hung. Of the man I know nothing, as I didn't happen to meet him, but he had a dissipated, *blasé* face, a type only too common among the foreigners in the East.

There was a great deal of hand-shaking and bowing and cigarette-smoking among this glittering little coterie, and a hum of conversation in all languages, much of it being sadly butchered. Suddenly a silence fell upon all. There was a distant sound of bugles, then the swelling notes of the national hymn, then a dashing line of carriages that sped across the field toward us. Two or three of them passed us and stopped just beyond the

The Mikado's Birthday

next tent. There was a whisper "Not yet! Not yet!" Then with a dash of outriders, the standard bearer of the royal sixteen-petaled chrysanthemum appeared, and just behind him, in a gorgeous carriage of state, sat the Dragon Eye, divine descendant of the Sun Goddess, the Mikado himself!

He is an emperor whom one can justly praise; interesting not only for what he represents, but for what he is, a man whose short life-time has seen almost miraculous changes in his country, changes for which his broad mind is largely responsible. He is the idol of his people and they blindly follow where he leads. During the war he went to Hiroshima, where he could have the first despatches from the scene of action, and lived like the commonest soldier, refusing fire and anything but the plainest food, sitting all day on a rough wooden chair, consulting with his advisers. When urged to take better care of himself he replied: "Should not I too make sacrifices when my children are suffering?" The empress also seems to be a rarely lovely character. She is widely charitable from her personal fortune, and while the emperor was at Hiroshima, she and the ladies of her court busied themselves preparing lint and bandages and visiting the wounded and dying. She also gave artificial limbs to all who had to have limbs amputated, to the Japanese and to the Chinese captives alike. Mrs. Nishigawa told me that years ago she had Miss Strickland's "Lives of England's Queens" translated into Japanese for her majesty; that it seemed to make a profound impression on her, and that she believed it had greatly influenced her life. The Japanese believe their emperor to have descended in unbroken line from the sun goddess who came down to earth some thousands of years ago, and no more than a generation back the Mikado was kept in a sacred palace in Tokyo, guarded by moats, and looked upon as a divinity. It was thought by the people that to look upon his face meant death. What a remarkable change there has been, then, that this monarch of the present day should review his troops, equipped with European arms, he himself dressed in a uniform of European style, with his people all around him.

There is always a double influence in a great review for me, exhilarating and the reverse. The music and the banners and the rhythmic beat of the troops are all inspiring, but I always think, with a shiver, of the wicked work those fields of shining spears could do, and of the bloody cause they really represent. It is a grim necessity that calls for all that brilliancy and that mechanical precision.

There were six thousand men out that day, and after riding around the field accompanied by his generals, the Mikado reviewed the troops, again got into his carriage, and, with another flourish, outriders and standard bearers and the gorgeous carriage were off, as they had come. I was disappointed not to see our Minister Dun at the review. He does not often go and was not there this year. Had he been present he would have been a conspicuous member of that beplumed and bedecked company, conspicuous for the lack of galloon and gold

THE PAGODA AT NIKKO

The Mikado's Birthday

lace, for the United States prescribes for a court costume the conventional black evening dress.

. . . .

That night we went to the ball. Minister Dun was there, by the way, and danced in the cotillon with a little Japanese woman not even so high as his heart. He is fond of a joke, and when I told him that he danced like a fairy he asked me what it was that I wanted him to do for me.

The grand ball was given at the Hotel Imperial, where we were stopping, so we were saved any awkward demand for evening cloaks and hoods which are not apt to be found in round-the-world trunks. As it was, the Wise One and I donned our prettiest evening frocks, which carried us through quite complacently. The ball was given by the Count Okuma, Minister of Foreign Affairs, and the Countess Okuma, in honor of the emperor's birthday. I don't know how we came to be honored with invitations, for they were not to be had for the asking. Probably it was that four or five yards of letter that we had to Mr. Montono. At any rate, the invitations came, written in French, asking that Monsieur, Madame and Mademoiselle Sweetser would do the Count and Countess Okuma the honor of passing the evening of November third with them, and announcing in small letters at the bottom that "L. L. A. A. J. J. les princes et les princesses, would honor the function with their presence!" It was quite an imposing document, I assure you, and for a time I was uncertain whether I would rather keep the invitation or go to the ball, for we were asked to present it on entering. It is just so with my Japanese passport. That passport is a work of art and I long for it as a souvenir. A footnote in English states expressly that unless it is returned I can never have another, but I have a mind to take the risk and keep it.

When we descended the stairs at the Imperial we passed through the brilliantly lighted vestibule, which was hazy with cigarette smoke and crowded with men, into the corridor. There we made a low bow to the count and countess and the line that stood receiving and followed the procession into the ball-room. There were two thousand guests, so you may imagine there was no time for a tête-a-tête. I had only a glimpse of the count and countess on entering. The count was an intelligent looking little man, and his wife a sweet-faced woman who looked weary and indifferent. She wore a white satin ball dress with a long train which did not suit her as her own graceful costume would have done. Some beautiful jewels blazed on her corsage, and on her head she wore a "ta ra ra" of diamonds, as Mr. O'Flannigan said.

The evening was one long feast of novelties to me, and though it isn't courteous to criticise one's entertainment, I couldn't help being amused at many things. A trip to the supper room was in the nature of a battle, and victory belonged to the strong. My first escort succeeded after some skirmishing in bringing me a biscuit and some cold salmon, with nothing for himself. A little later another captured some champagne and some sliced ham. There was an elegant and elaborate

The Mikado's Birthday

lunch served, if you could only get to it, and by dint of skillful combinations I finally fared very well. Some of the Japanese men made very comical mistakes trying to eat our food, and the rows of dear little Japanese girls looked woefully ill at ease sitting on the very edges of their chairs, sometimes two on a chair and evidently afraid of falling off.

My dance program included English, Australian, Portuguese, Italian, American and Spanish gallants and the conversations did some international gymnastics to which I am quite unaccustomed. It was great fun!

The princes and princesses came and went, sitting for a little while at the end of the ball room while the cotillon was danced. They were ushered in and out by the national hymn and ate supper in a special room reserved for them. The young princesses were very pretty in beautiful Parisian toilettes and lovely jewels.

That night I dreamed of a storm of red snowflakes against a pure white sky. They were the discs on the national flag that had danced in my eyes all day.

.   .   .   .

We came away from Tokyo at dusk when there was a faint yellow glow still left in the sky and a few dim stars peeping out. The streets were full of swift-flying fireflies, the lanterns the riksha men were swinging as they scurried along like little imps of darkness in the shadowy light. Along the moat the gnarled old pine trees stood out black against the sky bending toward one another at all sorts of tipsy angles. It was a fascinating Tokyo that we were leaving so regretfully. The twilight glamour had never been more potent. There is no telling to what length my sentimental mood might have gone, but just before I got to the station I caught sight of a last comical English sign, English as she is Japped, of which there is a rare collection in Tokyo—"Whatever goods sent into all directions," it said, and I laughed.

. . . .

One day we went down to Kamakura to see a big bronze statue of Dai Butsu or Buddha, said by the guide book to stand alone as a Japanese work of art, no other giving such an impression of majesty or so truly symbolizing the central idea of Buddhism—the intellectual calm which comes of perfected knowledge and the subjugation of all passion! The Kamakura Buddha's dimensions are forty-nine feet as to height and ninety-seven as to circumference, and I am sorry to say I thought him pudgy and uninteresting instead of intellectual, and was most disappointed because they wouldn't let me climb up and sit on his thumb, as they used to let people do, to be photographed. I suspect the guide book scribe of having copied his enthusiasm from somewhere else and I was more impressed by the wording of a notice to visitors put up by the bishop of the diocese. I wish I had copied it so that I might give it to you exactly, for it was a model of dignity, but I can only give you the idea. The grounds as well as the statue have been the victims of senseless vandalism committed by tourists, and the notice begs that the reader, whether

The Mikado's Birthday

Mohammedan or Buddhist, Jew or Gentile, of whatever creed, or tongue, or race, will remember that he treads upon ground hallowed by the true worship of ages and forbear from insult.

On our way to Kamakura we stopped to see a temple, and at the foot of the long flight of steps which always leads to a shrine we stopped to examine a lotus bed, so lovely in the summer, now in the sere and yellow leaf, and filled with great brown seed pods instead of blossoms. As we stood for a moment we heard a shrill sound of voices, and looking beyond, we saw a long line of little folk walking two abreast and winding toward us like a great serpent. It was a village school, the guide said, all boys, and they were singing at the very top of their lungs a spirited song, commemorating Japanese victories in the late war, first one division taking it up then the second answering, while the little fellows walked along swinging their arms and evidently enjoying the noise. They were very poorly dressed and the sight of our party nearly spread a panic of fun in the ranks, but they rallied when admonished by the teachers and wound along out of sight shouting more vigorously than ever on what I by courtesy call their song. They were long out of sight before out of sound, and all that day I would find myself smiling as I thought of those lusty little patriots and their howl for the fatherland. I needed a reserve of smiles, too, for the day was rather depressing. The glamour on Japan seemed to be getting thin in spots. We rode all afternoon through the villages. The people were the dirtiest and most repulsive that I have seen, though the district is prosperous and it is in their little huts that much of the fine Japanese silk is spun and woven. The Japanese use a great deal of hot water for bathing, but none of it by any accident ever seems to get on the children's faces. A visit to a district school that day left us no appetite for tiffin. Tiffin is the accepted word for lunch, and "to tiffin," "to have tiffened," "tiffened" is a verb in good standing.

That was rather a notable tiffin, too, for when we had been at the hotel for a few minutes our guide came and whispered to us, evidently impressed by the solemnity of the occasion, that we would be seated in the dining room at the table next to Mr. Henry Payne Whitney and Mrs. Whitney, née Gertrude Vanderbilt. They are a very prepossessing young couple, both good looking, conspicuous only for good taste and good manners, and apparently very fond of one another. Perhaps someone would like to know what Mrs. Whitney wore, so I'll tell. A dark blue gown trimmed with a Persian embroidery on corn colored broadcloth. Her collar had corn colored ribbon slipped under a turn-over collar of dark blue and tied in the back with a big bow of many loops and ends, and she wore a toque trimmed with blue corn flowers. She has a brilliant complexion and dark eyes and the toilette was very becoming to her.

I contrast the looks of Americans very favorably with those of other nations, particularly the Japanese, perhaps because I have my share of the colossal conceit with which I once heard our nation twitted. The young

The Mikado's Birthday

Japanese women are very often **pretty**. They are dainty little things, always with beautifully molded hands and arms, and often pretty features and complexions, to which their stiff, shiny, elaborately dressed hair gives a **final quaint** touch, but some of the men are the ugliest **monkeys** I ever saw, who support the Darwinian theory **to a** truly marvelous extent. Good Mr. Darwin **would** have revelled in "I told you so's" over here. However, I wouldn't for anything be ill-natured in my criticism of them and I have all admiration for their pluck and progressiveness—a courteous, cheery, industrious race who support their 40,000,000 inhabitants in a territory about the size of our California and who ask favors of no one. With many great evils in their social life there is much **good** and long may they wave.

I had heard before coming to Japan that it was changing rapidly, and supposed, without knowing, that it was because so many foreigners were coming in. Not a bit of it! In Tokyo, for instance, there are only about two hundred and fifty foreign residents all told, and the one store where European ribbons and laces and articles of dress can be bought would hardly grace a cross-roads. It is kept by a fat old Jap who doesn't speak a word of **English** and who sucks his breath through his teeth so **loud that you can hear him** across the street, and who **bows his nose to the counter every** other minute. Sucking the breath is a bit of politeness that takes the place of our handshaking and you **are** everywhere received with **a** prolonged S-s-s-s-s-s-s-s, accompanied by a grand kotow. It is the Japanese themselves who are so progressive and so eager to take up with the new. Everywhere, even in the little mountain hamlets, we see electric lights, and that is only one of a hundred evidences that the old, easy-going, gracious Japan is doomed and civilization is at its heels.

. . . .

It is my theory that the ideal traveler should be equipped, as to hand baggage, with a valise—not oppressively new, but of distinguished, well worn appearance—and an umbrella. Yet in spite of this firm conviction, I am usually provided in one way or another with about everything but a bird cage. By great strategy I managed to make my escape from Indiana with only a camera beside the ideal valise and umbrella. Pride goeth before a fall, and it came in Tokyo. I am now traveling with a pine tree! Not only have I a pine tree, but considerable landscape connected with it, a plat of ground and a moss grown rock, and I bought it all for fifty sen at the Shiba bazaar. My pine tree has great twisted roots that stand up well from the ground and run well into it, a sturdy veteran of the forest, and its gnarled branches have braved the blasts of many winters. It bends out protectingly over the moss grown rock, just as the pine trees along the emperor's moat reach down longingly toward the water. Its needles are fresh green and altogether it is as bonny a little tree as there is in Nippon. I say "little" because my pine tree is only six inches high, and the plat of ground is five by seven inches, and the moss grown rock is about as big as a pigeon's egg. Seriously, the little tree that stands on the table as I write, is one of the wonders of Japan, and I have given you its exact dimensions. The talent of these people for producing things in miniature is unique in the world. With infinite skill and patience they train the little shoots, giving them just a little earth, a little water, a little light, and twisting the branches into fanciful curves, just as they do the large trees, then, when after years of care they have produced a perfect miniature of a gnarled old tree, you may buy it in the flower market of the bazaar for twenty-five cents of our money! I am told that the Japanese, up to the time that the country was opened to the foreigners, seemed to make no connection in their minds between the time they had spent upon an article and the sum they asked for it. Their price depended solely on the excellence of the result. They have largely outgrown that, as tourists know, but the marvelous little trees may still be bought for a song, though they are the result of a world of time and patience. At the bazaar we saw cherry trees eight or ten inches high, heavy with pink blossoms, shapely little maples hardly a foot high in as gay autumnal foliage as any tree of the forest, pine trees two or three feet tall, twisted and bent with the weight of a hundred years, little orange and persimmon trees bearing fruit about the size of a hickory nut, baskets of blooming chrysanthemums whose longest stalks reared their flowery heads four inches. We haven't enjoyed anything more in Japan than these gardens in a nutshell, and in the very first one I fell victim to my pine tree. I thought I would keep it to

One Way Round the World

enjoy only while I was in Tokyo, and give it away when I left, but this evening when we started to return to Yokohama I felt quite unequal to leaving it behind. Even the Wise One counseled that it be brought along. If I grow any more attached to it, you may imagine me en route for America with my pinelet and landscape in one hand and my ideal baggage in the other.

A GARDEN IN TOKYO

VIII

Japan's Glorious Mountains

WE went from Yokohama by rail and tramway and riksha, to a lovely place up in the mountains called Myanoshita, where the scenery and the peasants suggest Switzerland at every turn. Indeed, there is no place in the country where we have been that the scenery is not beautiful and the people quaint and picturesque.

The tramway took us eight miles through a long winding village street, sometimes varied by avenues of bending pines, and when we got to the end, Odiwara, it was dark. A crowd of coolies were waiting for us, each riksha decorated with a bulbous paper lantern, and after tea at the tea house we climbed into the rikshas and started for Myanoshita, leaving the tea house girls bent double with polite bows and smiling "Sayonaras." We rode for several hours up the mountains before we saw the gleaming lights of the Fuji Ya Hotel. It was a strange experience for us, even in Japan, the black darkness, the half naked coolies, the swaying lights, the eerie shadows of passers-by, all armed like ourselves with big paper lanterns. The cool night breeze was invigorating, and there was a song of mountain torrents in the air. The great black slopes rose so straight around us that we had to throw back our heads to see the stars.

The Fuji Ya is a fine hotel with fine hot baths straight from boiling springs. The excursions that can be made in the neighborhood are legion. One day we went up to the Ojigoku pass and had a grand view of Fuji, just as the sun was sinking to the horizon. We started in a riksha over a road that was fiendishly rough for the first mile or two but it afterward grew better and we rode with more comfort. As we mounted above the timber line, we had a vista of gaunt treeless peaks that shone like silver in the sunlight. In spite of the metallic glint, they had a velvety, changeable tone which we discovered was given by waving fields of a sort of pampas grass that grows clear up to the summits. After we left the rikshas we dragged ourselves up the rockiest, steepest mountain path that we've yet met—three full miles at an angle of at least forty degrees. One of the big gulches, known as the Big Hell, was full of a sulphur formation and sulphurous steam was rising in clouds from fissures in the rock. High up toward the summit, we crossed a comparatively level spot where our guide warned us to follow exactly in his footsteps, and then went ahead, striking the ground with his staff to make sure it would bear his weight. The hollow crust resounded like a drum, leaving us in unpleasant uncertainty how far we should drop if it caved in. It is in this place that several too venturesome travelers have lost their lives. I have not yet felt an earthquake shock in this country, so talented in that line, and though I

Japan's Glorious Mountains

have had my head filled with enough gruesome tales of them to make me wake up o' nights with the shivers, I have really been wishing that Mother Earth would favor us with an experience. However, when I was walking across that slippery hollow apology for terra firma, the thought of those gigantic mountains swaying on their foundations, with little myself trying to stick to them, gave me such a start that I hoped that the interesting earthquake shock would be indefinitely postponed. A little later we crawled along the edge of a spongy cliff, where my bamboo staff sunk three or four inches in the vari-colored earth at every step, climbed a last short incline, and then glorious Fujiyama burst upon our view. We had seemed at the tip top of loneliness, but there stretched its lofty, silent slopes far above us, away into cloudland. The sun was not shining directly on it and there was a soft haze in the atmosphere that made the lower part of the cone a purplish shadow, and through which the upper diadem of snow shone dimly. A range of lower mountains hid the base of Fuji from our view, but just above them, bordering the purple shadows of the cone, lay bank after bank of fleecy clouds shining white and tipped with pinkish gold where the sun reached them, melting into delicate grays beyond his beams. Peerless Fujiyama! No wonder her countrymen adore and worship her. We haven't half appreciated her as yet. You will know that I was at least enthusiastic, when I tell you that I arose at 5 o'clock next morning to climb another mountain to see the Fuji in the opal tints of dawn.

One Way Round the World

We came down the mountain at a great pace that evening after our toilsome climb of the afternoon. It is such work to go up, up, up, as an old St. Nicholas used to say, but it is such fun to go down, down, down.

It had grown quite dark by the time we got back to the riksha men, and we whirled down the path at breakneck speed, shut in by the mountains which were turned into black walls, silhouetted in jagged lines against the sky as if laid on by some giant brush dipped in sepia. An occasional glowing eye, high up in the wall, told us of the charcoal burners at work, and we passed the twinkling lights of the Gold Fish tea-house.

We arrived with a flourish at the Fuji Ya, weary and jolted, and I was massaged by a weird, bald-headed, blind little creature who is still another of the curiosities of Japan. Massage is very popular here and the calling is reserved solely for the blind. In the evening you can hear them going along the street blowing a plaintive whistle that warns the people of their approach. My funny little old woman, a widow, I judge, from her shaven head, came into the room feeling her way and sat down Japanese fashion on the floor while she waited for me. When she began I let her pound me and snap my fingers and screw my ears as much as she liked, while I made mental notes of the process. It was soothing and not too vigorous and left me feeling quite refreshed, though I had had a couple of hard climbs that day. I paid the little old lady ten cents of our money with two and a half cents additional for "sake" money, and she went on her way well pleased. Sake, pro-

Japan's Glorious Mountains

nounced sahkay, is the favorite liquor of the Japanese, distilled from rice and usually served hot in the same tiny handleless cups as tea. It has a pleasant taste, not unlike sherry. They call a "tip" "sake-money," just as the French and Germans say "pourboire" and "trink-geld."

. . . .

Shidzuoka.

We have come here by train and sedan chair from Myanoshita and are lodged in a real Japanese inn, the "Daito Kwan." It is real fun, too, for one evening, and I am sitting on the floor in the absence of chairs, writing beside an artistic lamp that I long to carry away with me. The lower frame is blackened oak and the shade is a hexagonal affair of light strips of wood with paper pasted between the strips. The room is a model of neatness, cleanliness and order, with matting floors and paper screen walls and smooth wooden ceiling. The bed consists of a couple of heavy comforts laid on the floor, and on it lies a sleeping kimono, adorned with storks and dragons. I shall dispense with the pillow, which is a block of wood that looks like a section of a T rail, for I'm sure I'd wake with every muscle in my neck protesting against the outrage. In one corner of the room is a pretty washstand, with a little flat metal bowl, tiny mirror and bouquet of chrysanthemums, though the washstand is an innovation, for formerly prince and peasant alike washed in a public room. They have here a room which the Mikado once occupied, sacred and never occupied since. Over my head hangs a motto in Chinese characters which Suzuki copied and translated for me. "Behold Fujiyama, oh Honorable One," it says, for Fuji may be seen from the veranda; in the next room there is a wish for long life and prosperity for the occupant. The depressions for the fingers in my screens, which take the place of knobs, are of bronze daintily modeled, and decorated with the irrepressible mountain.

Fuji and the bay were lovely as we passed them this afternoon. The mountain had that same low-lying cloud across her slopes leaving the cone clear and cloudless and we saw her in all the changing tints of sunset and twilight. The sky across the bay was shell pink, against which the gray mountains stood out in divine harmony. It was almost Lake Leman, if the quaint fisher folk along the shore had been a little more modern and a little more Swiss.

We dined in the foreign annex of this Japanese establishment in what is supposed to be foreign style. If the Mikado is first in rank in this country, there is no doubt but that the butter is second. It and an antique unwashed teapot were old friends, I am sure, and there were other shortcomings too numerous to mention. In fact, I'm afraid we won't appreciate the cuisine of the Daito Kwan till we get something worse.

There is a racket going on around me now that bodes ill for sleep. These Japanese have absolutely no nerves, and no amount of nerve-wrenching clatter disturbs them. In some places we have noticed that the wheels of the rikshas were allowed to slip about an inch on the axle, making an irritating, clapping noise, and when we asked why they were made so we were informed, forsooth, that it was so they would make noise enough for people to hear them and get out of the way. These paper walls carry every sound in the building, and outside there is a vigorous picking of samisens, to which some girls are singing. The samisen is a popular musical instrument, played universally, though it is supposed to have been brought from Manila about 1700. It is a graceful instrument, not unlike the banjo, and while far removed from what we call melodious, it has a niggery twang that one grows to like. If there is any beginning or end to the strains they play upon it they disguise themselves effectually and the music seems to be a series of disconnected minor tones played without any regard for time or tune.

The singing is a wonder! It always reminds me of a remark an Englishman once made to an uncle of mine. The story has a spice of impropriety in it, but it passes on its merit. This Englishman was traveling in America and was sitting in the smoking room of a Pullman car when my uncle entered. He had a banjo in his hand, and they fell into a conversation on banjos and darkey dialect songs, on which my uncle found the Englishman much better informed than himself. Finally he asked him if he played the banjo and sang. "Yaas," drawled the Englishman, "I do sing a bit. Not that I have much voice, y' know, but people will stand some d—d bad singing, if you can only pick a banjo a little." The same is apparently true of the samisen, for the

One Way Round the World

Japanese endure a great deal of that kind of singing. The samisen one might grow to crave but the caterwauling, never! Their songs are a series of rasping squeaks with many sudden flights from D flat to G sharp and back to most anywhere. It is with difficulty that we can accept their melodies solemnly, and the rendition of some of our airs by native bands is excruciating. Foreign music is the swagger thing just now, and they will have it, but the tuning of instruments is a detail that they neglect.

Shidzuoka is noted for its delicate basket work, a marvel of beauty, and for the residence of the last of the shoguns, where the old man lives in lonely exile, never receiving anyone or going off of his estate. We admired the baskets and looked down on the residence from one of the templed hills. Fortunately, too, we didn't let our Tokyo experience satisfy us but went again to a chrysanthemum show. It was an exquisite collection with none of the stiffness of the Tokyo figures, but aisle after aisle of regal blossoms either growing straight or trained in ingenious shapes, offering a wealth of glowing color, a real corner of the garden of Eden where chrysanthemums bloomed. There were all colors and sizes and shapes, jinrikishas, Fujis, bridges, lanterns, bells, even a bicycle, but I liked best the great frowsly Paderewskian ones of which there was a large and beautiful collection. Kiku is the Japanese word for chrysanthemum, a word I wish we might adopt instead of our lumbering chrysanthemum so often misspelled and mispronounced. The seasons here are one round of

DRUM AND SAMISEN PLAYERS

blossoms, each lingering to welcome the next. In the spring the whole land is bright with clouds of pink cherry blossoms. Then come waves of purple wisteria and in summer the creamy lotus lifts its stately head above the ponds. In the fall the autumn leaves vie with the gorgeous decorative chrysanthemums in vivid coloring and even in the winter there are plum blossoms at Christmas time.

. . . .

At Nagoya we revelled in the finest cloisonné ware that we have seen, and dutifully visited more temples, but I am sorry to say the thing that lingers clearest in my memory about that interesting place is the large collection of ridiculous superannuated wooden high wheels that seem to have found refuge there.

We, ourselves, were great curiosities in Nagoya, and one small, solemn, round-eyed Jap ran all the way from the station to the hotel beside my jinriksha, exactly as our boys follow the clown in the circus parade, except that he took the matter very seriously and was evidently filled with awe and amazement. But the bicycles! They were made of old carriage wheels, I think, and were always mounted by Japs, usually wearing their clogs and invariably staring at us. They would come up behind us rattling like drays and steering a course of wild semicircles down the street that made us anxious for the life and limb of everybody in the street, ourselves included. No debonair rider of a crack safety ever gave a more reckless exhibition of the art of staying on.

. . . .

One Way Round the World

Anyone who wrote about Japan would do it a serious injustice if he left out a paragraph on babies. Babies are everywhere in evidence, particularly the street babies, surely the most cunning, captivating little folks in the world, when the dirt isn't so thick it is nauseating. In a country where they wear white for mourning, and put foot notes at the top of the page, and use paper towels and napkins and handkerchiefs, but do their bundles up in cloth, where vehicles turn to the left instead of the right, and the lock is in the jamb instead of the door, and they build the roofs of the houses on the ground before they begin the walls—in short where everything is topsy turvy—it isn't surprising that babies are carried on their mothers' backs instead of in their arms. Dressed in wadded kimonos just like their elders, except that they combine a few more colors of the rainbow, these roly poly little bundles of humanity are tied to the back of the mother or to a brother or sister, sometimes not much larger than themselves, by a long band of cloth wound twice around them and knotted at the belt of the person carrying them. There they hang contentedly to all appearances, for they rarely cry, gazing with wondering eyes at this queer world they've come to, or sleeping soundly with their poor little heads rolled back or over to one side so far that it seems as if their necks would break. If they utter any protest the mother begins a jarring step that bounces the baby up and down in a way that would make an American baby howl like a Comanche but which they accept as soothing. It seems they are endowed with that blessed lack

TAKING CARE OF THE BABY

of nerves that their parents have, for they are astonishingly good. When they are beginning to walk they seem to be always entertaining themselves, and have a business-like air that sits very charmingly on them. Perhaps they are really a good deal older than they look, for the race is small.

Even the smallest children have their heads shaved, occasionally all over, but more often with a tiny tuft left just above the forehead, or over the ear, or at the nape of the neck, for seed, as one witty observer suggests. Some of the babies have a round spot shaved on the crown and beyond this a circle of their fine baby hair stands out like a smoky halo. The older children have straight black wiry hair, cut in many fanciful designs according to the taste of their parents. Sometimes they have the round bare spot on the crown, with another oblong clearing just above the forehead. The girls begin to do up their hair as soon as there are wisps long enough to moor a couple of false puffs and anchor them with a hairpin. They cut the hair in front in a two-storied bang that hangs over the ears with lambrequin effect.

The pretty "geisha," or dancing girls, the sirens of the tea houses, do their hair in the most remarkable towers of shiny puffs decorated with many fancy hair pins, a style that makes the artificial little women look more artificial than ever. They powder their faces till they are chalk white, sometimes intentionally leaving patches of their yellowish skin untouched. One night at the theater I noticed a geisha who had three very pointed triangles on the nape of her pretty neck, painted, I supposed, in yellow, but I discovered that they were patches of her natural skin left unpowdered. I can't imagine how they manage to "draw the line" so neatly, for very often a band is left along the forehead next to the hair, as well. You can notice the same thing in the picture of the sacred dancers. The geishas' costumes are of the richest silks and crepes, exquisitely colored and combined, and though they wear no jewels, their toilettes often represent a small fortune.

SACRED DANCERS AT NARA

IX

Odds and Ends

THE position of woman is much inferior to that of man. She is sweet, gentle and obedient under many and peculiar trials, and is almost the slave of her husband. Miss Isabella Bird wittily remarks that what Japan needs to correct the evils of social life is, not to elevate the women, but to suppress the men. Another author who wrote a book on the customs of the country, which was translated into Japanese with a commentary, says they patted him on the back for many of his observations, but their wrath exploded when they reached his comments on the position of women. "The subordination of women to men," so runs the critical commentary, "is an extremely correct custom. To think the contrary is to harbor European prejudice. For the man to take precedence over the woman is the grand law of heaven and earth. To ignore this and talk of the contrary as barbarous is absurd." As the writer says, "it does not fall to every one's lot to be anathematized by half a dozen Japanese literary popes—and that, too, merely for taking the part of the ladies." The Japanese do not feel complimented either in private or public by praise of their women, their flowers or their art. It is of their progress, enterprise, business successes that they wish to hear. It is probable that they are so sensitive as to the position of woman, because they realize that it is the weak place in the grand march of progress of which they are so justly proud, and not being able to defend it they are easily touched by criticism. There is a little book called "The Japanese Bride" written by Rev. Naomi Tamura, published in Harper's familiar Black and White series, which I read some time ago, but failed to discover in it the elements of the tremendous sensation it created over here. The book showed that the position of Japanese women is in many ways deplorable, for they not only occupy an inferior position, but, as a rule, receive no inheritance from their parents, and may be divorced, and separated from their children also, for the most trivial causes, at the caprice of the husband. Divorce is very common, but fortunately a law is soon to be passed which is intended to remedy the abuse. The Rev. Tamura was accused, not of misrepresenting the state of affairs, but of telling too much about it, and he was expelled from the native presbytery of Tokyo. His loyal church followed him, however, and has been more prosperous than before.

"If the book had been written in Japanese for the natives," said his accusers, "with the intention of pointing out their defects to them, it would have been bad enough, but to hold up the faults of his countrymen to the gaze of foreigners was shameful and unworthy of a clergyman." The Rev. Tamura is a brilliant man, a graduate of Princeton and the Auburn Theological Seminary, and is well known in America where he has many friends, and any foreigner who reads his book

Odds and Ends

will be likely to acquit him of any disloyal intention in writing it.

Another book of the legion of books on Japan, one that I have found most interesting, is Mr. W. E. Curtis' well-named "Yankees of the East." It is written in a very attractive style and contains a mine of information well sugar-coated. Mr. Curtis did not spend a great deal of time in this country, yet his book is considered remarkably accurate by people who have lived here for years. In his opening chapter he urges "every man, woman and child of twelve years old and upward, who has the time and money, to visit the land of flowers and fans before its original picturesqueness is entirely overcast with the commonplace and colorless customs of modern civilization."

Mr. Curtis' chapter on "The Missionary Problem and Christianity from a Buddhist Standpoint" is particularly fair and helpful to any one interested in the great question of religion.

The work of the missionaries is very often strongly condemned, usually most strongly by people who have not investigated the subject at all. Even an unprejudiced observer, who believes that the Christian religion is best because it is the most elevating, is apt to decide superficially that the gate of paradise is much wider than our good ministers say and that it might be better to let these millions of people go happily to their Buddhist and Shinto places of peace whether they be called nirvana or heaven, undisturbed by the doubts and questions a new religion brings.

One Way Round the World

It is very difficult to reconcile religions when one takes the big world for a field. The differences of doctrine in the Christian church our missionaries find difficult to explain. "Why," say the Japanese, "you do not even agree among yourselves about your belief." This difference causes so much friction that missionaries of all denominations work largely together, and it is not unlikely that some time a single church will be established which will be known as the National Christian Church of Japan just as England has her Church of England.

As I say, a superficial observer might think that the labors of our missionaries in the field, the lives and the money spent, are not at all compensated or warranted by the results. Their work is too often sneered at by their own countrymen. But among those in a position to judge, the opinion is unanimous that the missionary influence has been a wonderful factor for good in the development of the new Japan. The work has always been encouraged and every courtesy shown by the highest officials of the empire, some of whom are Christians, and there are many flourishing native churches. The seed has surely been sown. When some one laughingly remarked to a prominent man, not himself a Christian, that our principal exports to Japan were kerosene and missionaries, he thoughtfully replied, "Yes, and both have brought us light, light for the eyes and light for the soul."

There is no Sunday in the Buddhist or Shinto religions, though they have some regularly recurring feast

A TEMPLE

Odds and Ends

days that are observed. My conscience is rather elastic, and I don't know that I should have remembered to go to church in Kyoto if the Wise One had not one fine morning reminded me that it was Sunday and taken me along with her. There were only a few worshipers, but we had a good Presbyterian service and sermon that carried us back home and made the Kyoto streets seem stranger than ever as we rode back to the Ya-ami. Another whiff of Indiana was in Osaka with Mr. and Mrs. B. C. Haworth. The guests besides ourselves were Dr. A. D. Hail, Miss Thompson and Miss McGuire, all missionary workers in various fields, and they entertained us with many accounts of their experience, some lively and amusing. The conversation was sparkling and the dinner—well, we had been existing at the Osaka Hotel and felt like the small boy who said he had swallowed a hole, and that dinner seemed to us the most delicious we ever tasted. Altogether it was a red-letter evening.

At the temples and shrines the worshipers write their prayers on a little slip of paper, then chew it into a wad and throw it at the big image of the god from whom they ask a boon. If the soft wad sticks they take it as an omen that the prayer will be granted, but if it falls they reason that they'd better pray again. It is hard for even the most dignified of gods to look imposing when irregularly covered with paper wads, and some of them are comical indeed. Sometimes the prayers are tied around the wooden supports of the images, and at one of the temples of Kwannon, the thousand-handed goddess of mercy, we saw a wall hung full of illustrated prayers painted on wooden blocks and others tied to the latticed screens.

Few of the waiters in the hotels understand English, and for convenience the dishes on the bill of fare are numbered both in English and Japanese numerals. You point to a number, the waiter looks at the corresponding one in Japanese and brings what you want. If you have learned to count "ichi, ni, san, shi," etc., you may add "ban," number, which, of course, comes after the numeral instead of before it in this land of reverses, and you'll have a pleased waiter and the satisfaction of speaking a little Japanese.

Over here the family name comes first, the given of Buddha name next, and Mr., Mrs. or Miss last.

The names of the girls are very fanciful and pretty. The empress' poetical name is "Springtime." Kiku, meaning chrysanthemum, is a favorite. One day I asked Suzuki, our guide, the name of his little girl, and he said it was "Ren," and that Ren meant brick. " 'Brick,' " I said in astonishment, for here was certainly a violent contrast to "Cherry Blossom," "Bamboo," "Silver," "Moonlight," "Perfume" and so on. "Why do you call a girl 'Brick'?" Suzuki is a good guide and he has saved us a world of annoyance and bother, but his English is occasionally very lame, quite paralytic in fact, and that was a notable instance of it. I gathered that he named the little girl Brick in consideration of the many admirable qualities of the brick, solidity, strength, immunity from destruction by fire and useful-

Odds and Ends

ness. "Beside," he said, "she was born near a brickyard." I am not sure whether this was an exceptional example, or whether, like our Indians, they sometimes name children from some circumstance, or event occurring at their birth or in their childhood.

One of the striking things in the instruction in the public schools is the cultivation of the spirit of patriotism. Of course, the late war has aroused all that was latent and a great wave of patriotism has swept over the land amounting almost to frenzy sometimes, yet it has always been a part of the Japanese education to cultivate a love of country. It is a great pity that there is not a more direct effort in that line in our own country where there is such a great need of assimilating our mixed population, and that our school boys and girls are not given object lessons in patriotism along with their arithmetic. In many of the small villages along the railway we have seen a procession of half the inhabitants out with banners and drums to welcome home a single private who had returned from his military service.

The Jap apparently has a great deal of misplaced confidence in his knowledge of English, and the results of a literal translation of the Japanese idiom into our language are intensely amusing. "Wine, beer and other," says one sign. "Patent shoes for iron bed," says another, meaning castors, I suppose.

Here is another set that I can vouch for as being actually in use. "Cigars, cigaretts, or A Ney (any) Kind." "Fresh Ox Milk." "Here one does dinner, and supper, coffee, tea."

One Way Round the World

This is an advertisement for fragrant Kozan wine: "If health be not steady, heart is not active. Were heart active, the deeds may be done. Among the means to preserve health, the best way is to take in Kozan wine, which is sold by us, because it is to assist digestion and increase blood. Those who want the steady health should drink Kozan wine. This wine is agreeable even to the females and children who can not drink any spirit because it is sweet. On other words, this pleases mouth, and therefore it is very convenient medicine for nourishing." And finally, a letter which Professor Chamberlain gives in "Things Japanese."

"Tokyo, Japan.

"Dear Sir,

"New year very happy. I salute prudently for your all. I had been several districts since July of last year. Now, here my head is mingled up with several admirations by the first voyage to abroad; but anyhow I feel very lionizing, interesting, profitable for experiment, by sailing about there and here. Though I exercised English diligently, yet I am very clumsiness for translation, dialogue, composition, elocution and all other. It is a great shamefulness, really, but I don't abandon English henceforth. I swear to learn it perseveringly even if in the lucubration.

"Tendering you my sympathy joy of your decoration, I am, Yours affectionally,

"M. L."

A SIGN IN TOKYO

Odds and Ends

It is all very well to laugh at these efforts, but I wonder if we should have as good luck in turning English into Japanese.

In Kyoto one day we were much amused at the sign of a practical life insurance company put up just outside the crematory. Suzuki first convulsed us by the way he sang it, chanting through his nose in a queer, droning fashion, just as all the Japanese read the Chinese characters that are used to print their language. In the train or in the stations it isn't unusual to see a line of half a dozen men singing the news to themselves, oblivious of one another. The list of the Chinese characters is endless and one must have a knowledge of three thousand, to correspond to our alphabet, and for printing a newspaper, for instance, at least five thousand are necessary; for the classics, ten, twenty, thirty thousand are required. The Japanese alphabet, which is printed beside the Chinese characters for the benefit of the ignorant, has forty-eight letters. It seems that the children are taught to sing the intricate Chinese characters and they can not understand them unless they speak them. Having the habit as children they keep it when grown and continue to sing.

The thrifty insurance company warns the reader that a cheery face and a healthy body are easily turned to a poor skeleton. People wither like the leaves of the forest and perish like the frail flower that trembles on the brink and is finally pushed into the abyss. Nobody knows what the future will be, and riches take wings. Finally, insure with this particular life insurance company and you will do a noble work in providing for your desolate family.

The Japanese refer to ne'er-do-wells and people who do not amount to anything, as "cold rice."

In bargaining with a Jap shopkeeper, if you wish to get a reduction you must not tell him that you are poor, but that you are rich. His reasoning is that if you are rich you are a prudent person who has saved his money by careful buying, and he makes the reduction.

The Japanese women "toe in" instead of out. Curly hair is considered very ugly.

Some comparisons with the Japanese are to the credit of the Chinese. Merchants in contracting with the Japanese require a bond with a heavy forfeit, but they consider the Chinaman's "Can do" as good as his bond.

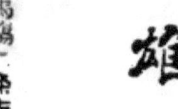

JAPANESE VISITING CARD.

Railway fares in Japan are graded to the purse of the traveler. First class, three sen a mile, second class, two sen, third class, one sen; a sen being one-half cent of our money.

The Japanese are so polite that their language, though rich in words, affords absolutely none for cursing and swearing. It took a breezy American to remark that though he admired that trait, he preferred his own land where they "kiss and cuss." Kissing as well as profanity is unknown in Japan.

X

In Palace, Temple, and Theater

AT NARA, we wandered happily along the lovely avenues arched over with fine old trees and guarded by rows of moss-covered lanterns, where the deer roam, timidly begging for the little cakes that are sold at the wayside booths and looking at us with great astonishment in their gentle eyes. They also recognized us as strangers. There is a wilderness of the graceful lanterns, row after row and vista after vista of them. Decidedly you mustn't omit Nara, and be sure to stop as we did at the Chrysanthemum Dewdrop, a quaint, delightful Japanese inn, so artistic and romantic that you will be a base ingrate if you complain of so sordid a circumstance as food. It was at Nara that we saw the painfully small holes cut in the pillars of the temples through which the faithful followers of Buddha manage to squirm, and it was also at Nara that we saw the sacred dance. It was given by some odd painted maidens, dressed in flowing robes of red and white, with their hair, which was elaborately decorated with wreaths of artificial flowers and metal pins, hanging down their backs. They waved bunches of tinkling bells while a couple of priests clapped some wooden blocks together and played a melancholy flute, and an older woman sat on her heels and picked the koto. After the dance was finished the girls displayed a very worldly interest in my famous velvet cape, and making an extra "offering" we took their pictures.

As we came at night into Osaka, the city, with its many rivers and canals reflecting the lights in long shining lances on the dark water, seemed to me an Oriental Venice, but the daylight showed it to be bustling and commercial, more like Rotterdam than the Bride of the Sea. It is an interminable distance from the station to the hotel, but I always enjoy the night rides thoroughly, with the narrow streets, the dark little latticed houses, the decorative glowing lanterns, the mysterious pedestrians, the flying rikshas, the open shops. In Osaka we called on our kind Japanese friend, Mr. Asai. Mrs. Asai is a dear little Japanese woman who does not speak a word of English, but she smiled and served us tea, sitting on the floor and holding a sweet Japanese baby who eyed us wonderingly but wasn't afraid of us. The house was a gem of simplicity and neatness, very little but matting and screens and delicately carved wood, an improvement in some ways over our elaborate style of furnishing. I suppose along with other nerve-wearing customs of hurry and enterprise which the Japanese men seem destined to gradually adopt, the Japanese women will change their simple method of housekeeping. Mr. Asai showed us all over the house, not from garret to cellar for there was neither, but through all the rooms and the pretty garden as well. He says that he remembers with what interest he studied the establish-

THE ENTRANCE OF A THEATER

In Palace, Temple, and Theater

ments of many courteous Americans, and that he is very glad to give those who care for it a glimpse of Japanese home life. Mr. Asai has fitted up an American room, just as we have our Oriental rooms, with grate and carpet and window curtains, which seem oddly out of place in the house, but are, of course, a source of great pride and satisfaction to him.

. . . .

Not in a volume could I tell you of all the fascinations of Kyoto.

"Tokyo people like eat," explains Suzuki. "No care much for kimono. Kyoto people like very much beautiful fine kimono, not so much eat." And it is true that we saw the gayest, prettiest costumes in Kyoto. There is a great rivalry between these two imperial cities, the Eastern and Western capitals, as they are called, and it appears that the point of dispute is the ladies' kimonos, instead of the size of their feet. Kyoto people feel much chagrined that the Mikado has taken up his permanent residence in Tokyo, and that the great palace in Kyoto is almost always closed. We visited two of the Mikado's palaces, both interesting, though the second was much more ornate than the first. The first stands in a great wooded park which once contained the residences of the nobles, since destroyed, I think, by fire. The history of these places is one long string of fires and floods and earthquakes, and it becomes a matter of wonder that anything is left. The guide-book, too, tells of vandalism which reigned at the opening-up of Japan, beginning with Commodore Perry's visit, during which a great many fine antiquities were destroyed in a senseless spirit of "progress." At the first palace, we entered at the Gate of the August Kitchen, and were shown around by a couple of distinguished looking Japs, in silk kimonos and peculiar wide pleated trousers, a good deal like our divided skirts, which are the conventional dress for visiting the habitation of the sacred Mikado, "*de rigeur*" in fact. European dress is allowed and Suzuki was out in coat and trousers. In the palaces I noticed in the Japanese a feeling of reverence. They talk at the top of their voices in the temples, and walk around examining everything with careless curiosity, but in the palaces they lowered their voices, and trod with a solemn, reverential air in the apartments the Mikado had occupied. In one room we saw a throne—of matting, of course—with two lacquered stools on which the insignia of the Mikado's rank, the jewel and sword, are placed. The hangings were of white silk with bold black figures, and were tied with bands of red and black, decorated with birds and butterflies. In one corner of the room was a square of cement, where night and morning earth is placed so that the Mikado may worship his ancestors on the soil, without descending to the ground. In another hall was another throne, the "Cool and Pure" hall it was called, but "Cold and Draughty" would be better. In all that palace there is no provision for fire or anything that we call comfort, and for all I know, the descendant of the Sun Goddess shivers over a few coals in his hibachi, or fire pot, warming his pulse and rub-

In Palace, Temple, and Theater

bing his hands just like the common people. The throne in this room was a beautiful chair with a back shaped like the torii, or gates that always stand in front of the temples.

At the Nijo palace, which used to be a part of the Nijo castle, now destroyed, we saw the most splendid apartments we have seen anywhere. The great Shogun Ieyasu lived there for a time and the suites of apartments, though somewhat dimmed by time, are still a blaze of golden glory. The screens are all covered with gold leaf and decorated by the "old masters" in the bold fanciful designs that we are learning to appreciate if not to admire. The ceilings, and indeed all the details, down to the small metal finishes, are marvels of delicate work. The whole has an effect of stately grandeur. The designs on the screens have the huge gnarled branches of the imperial pine, many of them life size, figures of herons and eagles, cherry trees in blossom, the kingly peony, chrysanthemums, tigers, bamboo, cats—all the designs dear to the Japanese heart, except Fuji. If Fuji was there it escaped me. How I should like to slip into those wide, silent halls some Halloween at midnight, when fairies dance and spirits waken, and see if the moonlight beams wouldn't reveal a shadowy shogun in all his old time pomp and magnificence, glistening with jewels, and surrounded by his prostrate vassals the daimyos—all the by-gone glitter and splendor the tarnished walls have seen, and of which they are a melancholy monument.

Japan has seen marvelous changes and I'm told that

many of the sons of samurai, the warrior class next in rank to the daimyos, are now riksha runners. One day I asked Suzuki if people looked down on the riksha men, because they do such menial work. "Do you, for instance?" I said. Suzuki shrugged his shoulders in a style that would have done credit to a Frenchman, and replied: "I no look down on riksha man. Maybe I pull riksha myself tomorrow."

The new temples at Kyoto are grand, indescribably rich in carving and gold and lacquer. The palaces attached have more of the gilded, grotesquely-decorated screens. As nearly as I can understand and express it in a few words, the Japanese idea of art is not to represent things as they are, for may we not enjoy them so in nature, but to convey an original idea by distorting the subject.

A trip to Lake Biwa is a charming excursion from Kyoto and affords the very novel experience of going on a canal through three tunnels in the mountains, one of them several miles long. It is a wonderful trip. Never, before Charon rows me across the river Styx, do I expect to feel as creepy as I did in that frail rocking little craft, creaking and groaning along that dark vaulted passage, with only the light of a dim lantern to pierce the eternal gloom, or the flaring ghostly torch of a passing boat to cast uncanny reflections on the damp walls. "You mustn't forget to think of an earthquake when you are inside," some one had told me, "for that is half the excitement." I didn't forget, and again I wished the interesting shock indefinitely postponed.

A THEATER STREET

In Palace, Temple, and Theater

There is an awesome feeling in piercing the heart of a great mountain, an oppressive sense of the stupendous weight that hangs over one's head, apparently about as securely suspended as Damocles' sword. I, for one, and the rest of the family for two, breathed a sigh of relief when we found ourselves again in warm daylight in the same old world instead of a lower region to which that black, silent passage seemed surely to lead.

The theaters in Kyoto are unique and we were fortunate to be there at the time of the Maple festival, when we had the opportunity of seeing many of the famous geishas. The plays and dances are very odd and incomprehensible, and of course everything is managed just as we do not manage it, but the scenery is made very pretty with paper blossoms and twinkling lights, and the costumes are elegant. At the theater they check clogs instead of hats, and the people sit on the floor in little square compartments, drinking sake and smoking, with an occasional glance at the performance. Men and women both smoke a peculiar pipe, made of bamboo tipped with metal, which has a bowl about the size of a baby's thimble and only allows two or three good whiffs.

It is in Kyoto, as I told you, that fascinations never end. It is the most Japanese, the most interesting of all. If your interest in the sights flags, there are always the enticing shops, and one is apt to fall among shopkeepers when starting out with the most praiseworthy intention to visit the temples. If it isn't satsuma ware it is embroidery, or cloisonné, or bronzes, perhaps porcelain, silks, ivory carvings, curios, bamboo ware, anything and everything that is beguiling.

We lived most pleasantly at the **Ya Ami, a big** rambling hotel, beautifully situated on what is known as the Eastern Hill of the quaint city. One sunny morning we came sorrowfully away, followed by a last violent s-s-s-s-s from our faithful little waiter. Leaving the Ya Ami was very melancholy indeed, and the Osaka **Hotel only deepened the gloom.** It was the changing beauty **of** the Inland Sea that consoled us.

. . . .

On board the "Yokohama-Maru."

We sailed away from Kobe on the "Yokohama-Maru" for Shanghai. The Wise One thinks it is high time that we were leaving Japan when the head of the family expresses a desire to take a couple of little Japanese maidens home with him.

It was Thanksgiving day and we came out to the "Yokohama-Maru" in an open sampan, in a dismal downpour of rain, and ate Thanksgiving dinner on board, thankful that we hadn't **been drowned and that** we could eat.

The last part of the **voyage has been** fearfully rough. The ship is lying in the trough of the sea and we seem to be traveling faster sideways than we are ahead, in a series of horrid wriggly rolls. The favored few who have been able to appear at the table have with difficulty kept themselves on their **chairs,** and the **cook** has with even greater difficulty kept the **food on the stove.** I barely manage to stick to my chair and my subject.

In Palace, Temple, and Theater

Such weather is very bad for the disposition, very apt to make one want the earth.

We left Japan so regretfully. I rub my eyes and look at the broad Yellow Sea with the feeling that I have waked from a bright colored dream, too soon past. Come one and all to Japan when you would leave hurry and worry behind and dream the days away in lovely mountain districts or in the busy, crowded, curious cities among a kindly, smiling people, never too hurried to be polite or to render a service and always alive to the beautiful in nature and in art.

There are flaws, there always are, and it may be they would grow more apparent with time, but if you have a grain of leniency in your nature, you will forgive them all when you are holidaying, and agree with me that Japan is charming and not overrated, as some people say.

To-night I went up on the bridge to have a good view of the phosphorus in the water. I had heard of its wondrous glow in these eastern seas, but I could not have imagined anything so strangely beautiful. From the vessel to the horizon the sea is one sheet of gleaming, dancing lights that tip the crest of every wave and glow in a strange bluish fire where the foaming water dashes back from our cleaving prow. It is a veritable fairyland where all the sea sprites must hold high carnival. Beyond lies China, the unknown.

XI

In Old Shanghai

THE "Yokohama-Maru" slipped over the bar into the Yang-ste-Kiang with only six inches of water to spare. We had been afraid we would miss the tide, though Captain Swain had promised to send us up to Shanghai on a tug if we did. "You don't dare make it any closer than that, do you?" I said to one of the officers. "That is very close indeed," he replied, "and the ship will hardly answer the rudder, but I'll tell you a secret. I think we would risk it with even a shade less when Mrs. Swain is in Shanghai."

The "Yokohama-Maru's" officers are so agreeable that we left her with regret, even after that terrific shaking up that she gave us. I parted sorrowfully with the captain's pup, a lively, bright-eyed little fellow, with teeth like needles and a pup's characteristic inclination to chew everything he can find. I spent a good deal of time on his neglected education, trying to teach him to bring me a handkerchief, but he looks upon life as a joke and was loath to accept responsibilities.

The broad Yang-ste-Kiang is yellow and muddy like the Yellow Sea. Shanghai, with its smoking stacks and foreign-looking buildings, has nothing Chinese about it from a distance, and if it were not for the pic-

A SHANGHAI CAB

In Old Shanghai

turesque river craft on the Yang-ste, junks and sampans with a big round eye on each side of the prow, you might think you were coming into Chicago. The crowd at the dock would dispel that illusion. They do the least with the most noise of any crowd I ever saw. The process of landing is like a true Irish debate, everybody talking and nobody listening. The men wear roomy garments of blue denim and tie their little felt caps on with their queues. One of them is apt to offer you a ride on a "licensed wheelbarrow." The wheelbarrow is a favorite mode of locomotion among the lower classes, and they spin along the Bund side by side with the more aristocratic rikshas and carriages. They have a big wheel, on which the weight rests, are pushed by a man, of course, and are divided in the middle by a little railing. It isn't unusual to see a family riding on one side with a pig strapped on the other—a heavy load for one coolie, and he walks with a queer tottering gait that is painful as he balances the lumbering barrow. Sometimes they are very unevenly loaded and must be very hard to manage.

The rikshas have swelled and the lanterns have shrunk. In fact, we are in a new, totally strange country, and must focus all over again—excuse the photographer's term—in religions, traditions, race, customs and costumes. I'm surprised to find the Chinese men so much more attractive than the Japanese. They are a much finer race physically, much more intelligent looking and their dress is both more comfortable and more picturesque. There is a crudeness of coloring in things Chinese, but among the well-to-do the rich brocaded fur-lined garments of the men and the elaborate embroidered head dresses and jackets and trousers of the women are very beautiful. We all liked Shanghai. It is gay and cosmopolitan, a curious mixture of the familiar and the strange. Along the Bund, the street facing the harbor, are the concessions made by the Chinese government to the different nations, and you may see every flag from the tri-color to the Union Jack floating in the breeze. There is no general city government, and each concession has a post-office and is guarded by policemen of its own nationality.

The most picturesque figures of the street are the policemen of the English quarter, the tall, dark-skinned, fierce-looking Sikhs from India, of whom the Chinese stand in wholesome awe. They wear a dark uniform, but their heads are enveloped in a huge red or vari-colored turban as big as a keg. We stayed long enough to become familiar with the streets and to fall victims to the brocade and the silver dealers in the Honan and Nanking roads. All the streets in the city are called roads. The silver, too, is crudely chiseled compared with Japanese work, but it is very curious and pretty. One of my purchases was an odd big silver lock that I had seen the children wearing. It was attached to a hoop that hung around the neck, and I learned that the hoop was locked so as to keep away the evil spirits. Sometimes they put earrings in the boys' ears to make the evil spirits think they are girls. Girls are not worth their attention it seems. The Chinese brocades are ravishing, rich heavy silks that stand alone and to be bought for a half or a third of what we pay for them at home. Fur, too, is tempting, for it is very cheap, particularly a fine quality of fleecy Angora. The "tailors" who waylay you at the Astor House will make anything from street dresses to party capes and do it very well. They always come to the hotel to bring samples and fit you, and they will copy anything you give them exactly. One day I had occasion to look my tailor up at his place of business. Never shall I forget the dirty little hole in the wall that was his establishment, and I marvel that anything white ever came out of it. It is always so in China, and if you are pleased with results you should by no means inquire into the causes.

One night we went to see some opium smokers in what I suppose would correspond to a café in France. The process was new to me. We went into a dimly-lighted room where men were lying on divans either busy preparing their pipes and smoking them or dreaming the hours away in lazy content. There was a pungent, disagreeable odor in the air, the smell of the opium. It is a pasty, dark substance that comes in little porcelain pots, and the smoker very carefully melts and rolls a bit of it into a pill which he finally sticks on a peculiar flute-like pipe by means of a long pin and smokes it over a small lamp. "Hop" they call it. "No good for me," said one man we were watching, who knew a little English and was quite talkative.

After we left the opium smokers we went to a Chinese theater, where I saw all the devils and hobgoblins of my imagination, in the flesh. The house was full of well-dressed men and women, chatting and smoking, and immediately on our arrival a courteous attendant offered us each a steaming wet cloth to wash our faces with. We declined with thanks and turned our attention to the play. The orchestra furnished a crash of shivering discords that never for one instant ceased, and there seemed to be plenty of action in the plot. Time is money and money is silver, and as silver is depreciated in China it may account for the depreciation of time. Skits and curtain raisers last about six weeks over here, and they go to their plays by the year. In this particular one the make-up of the principal characters would have frightened a small child into fits. One of the ogres had his face painted in blue and white stripes, like the tennis flannels that used to be popular, and his glassy eyes rolled around in a way to make you shudder. There were some really clever acrobats who jumped about in curves rivaling the twists of the Chinese characters. They were bare to the waist and elicited the greatest applause by springing high in the air and falling to the bare floor, alighting on their shoulders with a thud that it seemed would break every bone in their bodies. They were finely built, muscular fellows, and I suspect that they have discovered the secret of turning into India rubber.

Another day we went over to the Chinese Shanghai, the old part within the walls. They say that it is one of the worst cities in China, and I breathe a prayer that it may be so. I can not imagine a place more liberally

CHINESE ACTORS

In Old Shanghai

and thoroughly frescoed with filth. There is no denying that many of the Chinese are dirty, foully dirty. There is some excuse for it, though, for the struggle for existence with them is pitiful. Ten silver cents a day; five cents of our money—so many cash they call it—is a princely income to many of them. All their dealings are in cash, the copper coins with holes in them that they string and wear around their necks. At the present rate of exchange you get a thousand odd cash for a silver dollar. In the interior, bank notes are unknown, and if you haven't Mexican dollars, you can carry a bar of silver and break off pieces as you want them. You may even pay your hotel bill with bricks of tea dust. The inconvenience of these methods doesn't appeal at all to the Chinese mind.

The streets of the native city in Shanghai are narrow and dark and tortuous, a maze through which you couldn't possibly find your way without a guide. On a rainy day the water would drip from both eaves on your umbrella. A narrow sedan chair can be carried through them, but it is a squeeze that discommodes the entire street, and the coolies have to go to a corner to turn around. The houses crowd so close together that "they leave for the eye's comfort only a bare streak of blue," and there must be many places which the sun's rays never find. The shops are curious as ever, and I was relieved to find the carpenters sawing away from their toes once more. We were interested, too, in the many fanciful green jade ornaments, a favorite with the Chinese.

One Way Round the World

We visited a joss house, burnt some joss sticks and offered up a string of silver paper prayers, by putting it in an oven built for that purpose. The Chinese idea is that anything which is burned is converted into air and reaches the gods. At their funerals they carry any quantity of eatables in the procession. The gods are supposed to feast on the odors, and the mourners regale themselves with what is left. In one procession I saw at least a dozen roast pigs, each one swung over the shoulders of two coolies, and tray after tray of cakes and other eatables.

I mustn't leave the subject of the old city before I tell you about the smells. It would be a sad injustice to the most striking features to leave them out. They are far too vivid, though, to do justice to in black and white. Yet we are told they are hardly noticeable now compared with what they are in summer! You may have lived a happy, untroubled life in which you have never had to classify smells, but you would come to it in China. There are smells and smells. Some smells are bad, but you feel that they may be good for you. Some are hopelessly bad. This is the kind that flourishes in the Flowery Kingdom! Take the extreme opposite of the odors of Araby; condense them; and you will have an approximate of the foul stench that assails your nostrils as you walk in Chinese streets. The subject gets to be a joke with travelers. If we didn't laugh about it we would surely weep.

I remember that a friend who has made this trip wrote me that he was trying to lay his hand on a Chinese guide-

In Old Shanghai

book that he had seen advertised somewhere, and that he would try to get it in time to reach me at Shanghai. "If I do not," he said, "I shall have to leave you to tackle the smells unaided." The guide-book failed to appear in the Shanghai mail, and his vigorous expression of my fate comes back to me with full force. The smells are awful.

There is no guide-book for China, at least none that we have been able to find, and we shall be at the mercy of guides for information. Shanghai is set down on the globe trotter's itinerary as a place where there is nothing to see. That must mean that there is nothing which can not be seen in other places, for there is so much that is novel and interesting. I shall remember it as the place where we first saw the poor, tortured little feet of the Chinese women. The custom is much more prevalent than I had supposed, and it is really unusual here to see a woman whose feet have not been bound. Their feet differ a good deal in size, but the soles of some of the smallest shoes are actually not more than two and a half or three inches long. When they are as small as that the women can hardly stand alone and have to be helped when they walk. What a singular custom it is. There is something repulsive about it, too, as well as painful, something hoof-like and animal about the stumps enclosed in the little pointed embroidered shoes. The women are really crippled for life, and once done the mischief can not be remedied even if they wanted to remedy it. There is a horrible fascination about the tiny misshapen feet, and for

One Way Round the World

the first few days, whenever I saw a woman hobbling along, I would always find my eyes riveted on her feet, wandering just how they have been distorted and what the real shape of the foot was. In Wen Chow (this is anticipating, but I'll tell you about it now) a pretty young Chinese girl showed us her foot, something that they very rarely do, so I can describe it to you just as it is. It was a shocking sight, and not one that one would want to see twice.

The foot-binding is one of the time-honored customs of the country in many provinces and in that way interesting. An appeal was once made to the emperor to forbid it, but he replied that it was a custom of his people with which he could not interfere. Truly fashion is more mighty than emperors. One of its vagaries was the style of extremely pointed toes which has just had its rise and fall in our own enlightened country. They were as far removed as they well could be from the natural shape of the part of the human form divine which they were intended to cover.

Nga Chiae pulled off her tiny embroidered shoe, then slipped off a kind of cotton stocking, shaped like the shoe. Then she deftly unwound the bandages that had bound the foot and kept it from development. You would have hardly recognized the member as a foot. When it was small and pliant, the small toes had been turned directly under the sole leaving only the great toe free, and it is the great toe that fits in the point of the shoe. The heel is abnormally developed and stands out from the front part of the foot like the heel of a

A CHINESE FAMILY OF WEALTH

In Old Shanghai

heavy boot. Above the little shoe where the instep is free there was an ugly knot that looked almost as big as my fist. I suppose that lump rises up because the body is thrown so far out of equilibrium. When the girl stands, her full weight rests on the heel and the narrow pointed foot and great toe, under which the other toes are bent. What a wicked, wicked thing it seems to deform and distort a child's healthy little foot until it becomes a hideous monstrosity like that. The little girls cry for two years with the pain. Yet the Chinese retort that their fashion of compressing the feet is no stranger than ours of compressing the waist, and is not nearly so harmful to the health. *"Chacun a son gout,"* as a Frenchman would say.

XII

A Week in Wen Chow, China

IT was the "Poo Chi" that carried us from Shanghai to Wen Chow, for a visit with Dr. and Mrs. Hogg, our good English friends of the "Doric." "Poo Chi" means everlasting affluence, I believe, and there is an affluence of good will and good cheer aboard her that makes her well named. Captain Froberg is a tall, handsome fellow, as genial as he is good looking, one of nature's noblemen. He is a Swede; the first engineer is a Scotchman, the first officer is an Englishman and the second officer is an American. They tell me that nearly all engineers are Scotch, and Mr. MacGregor says that if you stick your head in any engine room and sing out, "Hello, Mac!" you are sure to get an answer. Mr. MacGregor was the fourth passenger, a wonderfully well informed Scot who, I am sure, could tell me a great deal more about the United States of America than I could tell him.

These sailors spin the most entertaining yarns, whether they are sitting on the capstan or at the dinner table, and Miss Landlubber is picking up a pocket dictionary full of nautical terms and a volume of good stories. For instance, a "wind jammer" is a sailing vessel, and on the stories I wouldn't venture to begin.

CHINESE COFFINS AWAITING BURIAL

A Week in Wen Chow, China

One doesn't have to go far inland to see the real China, practically unchanged, and Wen Chow forty miles up the Ou river has little that is jarring in the way of modern improvements. The trip down from Shanghai is delightful, and I don't know why Wen Chow shouldn't be on the good books of sightseers as well as out-of-the-way Canton. The "Poo Chi" threaded her way among the islands just off the coast, and in many places the scenery is as lovely as in Japan's Inland Sea. The water, though, is yellow and thick with mud, and the sails of the junks, with an eye for harmony, are a rich tobacco brown. The mountain sides are checkered with fields and striped with rows upon rows of tombs. China is one great graveyard and the Chinaman's first duty is to worship at the tomb of his ancestors. In the angles of the old battlemented wall around Wen Chow we saw numerous coffins containing bodies, which were put there, we were told, until the relatives of the deceased could get enough money to bury them with the ceremony they desired.

The few days spent with Dr. and Mrs. Hogg and Mr. and Mrs. Soothill in their pretty homes at Wen Chow, are never to be forgotten—days to mark with a white stone, as Du Maurier says. The lives of these cultured, charming people, who have given up home and country to perform a labor of love among the degraded and suffering Chinese, are an inspiration to the most thoughtless. It is an atmosphere of which one breathes deeply as one does of a cool, bracing wind.

Our stay was one round of tiffins and dinners and

pleasure excursions. Wen Chow hadn't been so gay for a year, they said. One morning we went far up the river on a house boat, carried by an obliging tide that turned around in the afternoon and brought us back again. The captain was host that day, the weather perfect, the tiffin irreproachable and embellished by some of Li Hung Chang's champagne, at least some that was ordered for the "Poo Chi" when the viceroy's suite made a trip on her. We landed at several of the Chinese villages along the banks, where I attracted as much attention as one of Barnum's freaks. The women examined my gloves wonderingly, and when I took them off were lost in admiration of my fair, soft hands—fair and soft compared with theirs. The Chinese women, as well as the Japanese, admire a fair skin, and as nature never supplies them with one they use powder liberally. That day they even turned up my dress skirt to examine the lining and the underskirts. The houses of the villages were squalid and dirty—no more, however, than I have seen in other parts of the world. We had a lively time finding our way back from one place to the landing, though it was in full view all the time. The narrow paths skirt the rice fields, in which the water is very wet, and the fields are laid out with about the same regularity as the patches in a crazy quilt. In some places buffaloes were drawing a primitive plow made of a bent piece of wood; not our bison that we call buffalo, but a queer scant-haired animal that is much more like itself than anything else that I can think of. Their coat, or lack of it, made me think of a Mexican hairless dog.

A Week in Wen Chow, China

Buffalo milk, by the way, is the only kind to be had in Wen Chow, and it and the butter made from it are rich and good.

The streets of the city were narrow and smelly and crowded and noisy, though full of life and interest, and after a morning or an afternoon in them we would step into the restful flowery "compound" with a sigh of relief. Compound is the odd name given to the walled enclosure in which foreigners live. One day we called at the house of a rich merchant where we made the acquaintance of the whole family and were shown all over the house, a palatial one for China. The dog and the baby were afraid of us, and though they became somewhat reassured, they eyed us with trepidation to the last. Tea was served in cups with lids, and some delicious sweet cakes made of small oily seeds. The cup must be taken with both hands—it would be a gross breach of etiquette to take it with one, and it is also *au fait* to extract the tea between the lid and the cup without taking the lid off. There is a suggestion for 5 o'clock tea enthusiasts along with the three-cornered cup and souvenir spoon inflictions. Not that I object to the beverage that cheers but not inebriates, but to the impossible cups and spoons.

Another time we received a call from a Chinese mother and daughter. They were elegantly gowned, I should say jacketed and trousered, and I wish you could see their calling cards, a style to delight an anarchist, flaming red with big black characters. The ladies arrived and were carried away in sedan chairs, swung by two poles on the shoulders of coolies. We often rode in them ourselves, but I always preferred to walk. They crowd the streets so badly and make it very uncomfortable for the pigs, poor things, for they have to get out of the way too, and do so hate to do so. I've seen many a porker assisted squealing on his way, and once I had a dog fight right under my chair. The Chinese remarks that filled the air must have been intense to a degree, but fortunately, I didn't know them from quotations from the Bible. The Chinese have not the innate courtesy of the Japanese, and it is just as well sometimes not to know what they say.

One evening just at dusk we saw a bride dress for the marriage ceremony which was to take place several miles in the country. When we went into the room she was dressed in a long robe of green and black, and over this the wedding garment was slipped. It was a gorgeous affair of red and gold, and on her head they put a heavy head-dress of what looked like our artificial flowers. They were carved out of wood, however, painted and gilded. The bridegroom's gift to the bride is a hairpin, which she wears at the wedding. Her trousseau is carried ahead of her in red wooden boxes. Red is the color for weddings and white is the color for mourning.

The bride was a sweet-faced, very young girl. When she came out of the house to get into the chair she had a square of red cloth thrown over her head and head-dress. The head-dress is enormous, so it had a most grotesque effect.

A Week in Wen Chow, China

The bride's parents do not appear at all at the wedding, but are supposed to stay at home and weep. The poor little lonely bride, who is often to be married to a man she has scarcely seen, gets into a gorgeously decorated sedan chair, a box-like affair that must be far from comfortable, and the door is locked and not opened until the bridegroom unlocks it at his father's house.

Sometimes in the hot summer weather the head-dress is so heavy and the veil so stifling that the girl faints in the chair. The chair we saw was decorated with many candles placed so recklessly near the inflammable decorations that I felt anxious for our little bride's safety.

The marriage procession is as elaborate as the means of the parties will allow.

There are lantern bearers and musicians who wear red jackets and carry big fans. There are usually bridesmaids, except that they are not maids but middle-aged women, and the resplendent chair is carried by four ragged coolies very much out at the elbows.

Nothing is ever done quietly in China, and there is a vast amount of shouting and arguing done before the procession is finally off.

The ear-splitting music either accompanies the din or drowns it altogether, and the fire-crackers crack merrily. At the marriage there is feasting for several days.

We came away from Wen Chow with a tremendous snapping of the fire-crackers which hung in long strings in the "compound" and at the dock and were carried in front of us through the streets—not in our honor, I must explain, but in honor of Mr. and Mrs. Heywood, who, after five years of good missionary service at Wen Chow, have been called to the field in Ning Po, and came away with us. There was a crowd of natives at the dock to see them off, and the tears in many eyes were a touching tribute to the love and esteem in which Mr. and Mrs. Heywood were held.

"Good-bye, heart of the river," said little Frank Heywood in Chinese, for he chatters Chinese with his amah faster than he can English with his mother.

"Good-bye, heart of the river!" He was looking at the island, with its two sentinel pagodas.

"Good-bye, heart of the river," said I, as I answered the signals of the little group of fluttering handkerchiefs on the docks till they grew so small that they looked like butterflies dancing in the sunlight. "Good-bye, Wen Chow!"

I had left a part of my heart there in good keeping.

XIII

In the China Sea

WE are on board the "Rohilla," bound for Hong-Kong. She is a stanch vessel of the Peninsular and Oriental Steam Navigation Company plying between Shanghai and Bombay, and affords another of the swift transitions of which the Orient is full. Just as we were becoming accustomed to the Celestial, with his yellow skin, almond eyes and garments of rich brocades, we find ourselves among dark-skinned, red-turbaned East Indians—nor is that all. The crew of the "Rohilla" is a curious mixture of nationalities. Not a pig-tail in sight. The captain, chief officers and stewards are conventional Englishmen, the waiters are a mixed Portuguese and Indian blood called Goanese, the stokers are Punjaubers from the Punjaub district in India, the sailors are picked up around Bombay, and the coal trimmers are thick-lipped Africans from Zanzibar.

I said not a pig-tail in sight, but there is one, belonging to a passenger, Tong Saey Chee, who is going with his family to Hong-Kong. Tong is what is known as the compredor of a big Russian tea house. A compredor is a middle man between the native producers and the foreign buyers, and it is he who gets the biggest "squeeze." Tong is evidently very wealthy, and his family wear the most elegant clothes we have seen. They are dressed in Chinese fashion, but the wife has enormous sparkling solitaires in her ears and the little girls have big stones with strings of pearls hung from them. The son is a sturdy, fine-looking boy, and his father tells me he is only eight years old. The feet of one of the little girls are so small that her amah has to help her when she walks. She wears the elaborate embroidered band around her head and her hair is all drawn to one side just over the ear and braided in one braid that is finished with a long heavy crimson silk tassel. She is a friendly little thing—they all are—but I can only talk with the father, who knows a little pidgin English.

All grammar abandon, ye who learn pidgin. I'm afraid I haven't yet mastered the subject, but I can give you a few examples of it. Pidgin is supposed to be a corruption of the word business, though I think that derivation rather a strain on one's credulity. In the first place, a means of communication was necessary between foreigners and the Chinese, and besides, the dialects of the different provinces in China are so dissimilar that though the written language is the same the people can not understand one another. A man from Ning Po can not understand a man from Wen Chow, yet they are not a day's steamer-ride apart. If you ask a Shanghai boy on the boat to buy something for you in Ning Po he will say, "No can buy, no sabe speak."

This pidgin language that has sprung up is used between English and Chinese and oddly enough between the Chinese themselves when they can not understand one another in their own language. It seems to be a simplified English, with superfluous words weeded out and the most prominent words put in the most prominent place. Some of the funniest expressions are said to be a literal translation of the Chinese idiom. John calls a side wheel steamer an "outside walkee" and a stern wheel an "inside walkee."

"Piecee" is a favorite word. The first officer of the "Doric" was known as the first piecee mate. When we went up the Ou from Wen Chow we told the boy who served as master of ceremonies that we wanted to go to where three piecee river came together. You give an order something like this: "John, go topside and tell one piecee gentleman I want see him." Topside is up on deck or upstairs.

When there is a no in the sentence it usually comes first and a Chinese will always answer yes to a question whether he means yes or no. "Can do," or "No can do," says the tailor. "Have got," or "No have got." "My no sabe." When you are calling and want to know if a gentleman is in—"Boy! Master have got?" "Yes," he will answer, "Master no have got."

Chop chop is fast and chin chin is a word that means a sort of congratulation or greeting. Chow is food and chit is a card or bill. Sabe is to know or understand. "Boy! No wantchee wait, wantchee go chop chop to hotel." The food at the hotel is known even among Europeans as the chow, and you are told by people who are circling in the opposite direction from yourself what you may expect in the way of chow further on. There is a certain hotel where the chow is notoriously bad, but which is always full, because it is the best in the place. "What can you expect?" said a Californian. "If I had such a cinch as that I'd feed my guests on rosin." Squeeze is the expressive word for a commission, and every Chinese in the empire except the last one squeezes somebody beneath him in rank or position.

There are always big painted eyes in the prow of a boat. "No have got eye, no can see, no can see no can sabe," reasons the sailor, and he really believes it. It is a good joss, good luck, for a small vessel to cross the bow of a large one, and that superstition gives the captains of the steamers no end of trouble and annoyance. The man in the small boat thinks that the evil spirits which are ever following him will swarm to the large one when he crosses its bow. Chinese boys do not climb trees because they are afraid of the evil spirits of the air.

. . . .

Hong-Kong, meaning good harbor, is as beautiful as it is good. I shall never forget it as I saw it first one bright morning. The "Rohilla" came into port at night, so we did not stand on deck watching the gray line of land rise and widen into hills and valleys and plains and the microscopic buildings grow to the size of human habitations as we probably would have done in day-time. Instead, we stepped out on deck in the morning to find ourselves lying in water as blue as a sapphire, surrounded by stately ships, with Hong-Kong

CHINESE JUNK, SHOWING THE EYE

In the China Sea

rising in terraces in front of us away up to the Peak, over which there hung a filmy cloud. The city made me think of a honeycomb, for the houses are all built with rows of stone verandas with arched openings which give exactly that effect at a distance. Now that I know Hong-Kong well and have sauntered often in its busy, picturesque streets and along the leafy, fresh green paths that line the hillside, I've grown to think it one of the most beautiful places I've ever seen. The view from the Peak over the harbor and sea is enchanting. You are hauled up there by a remarkable tramway which slants at an angle that I would not venture to guess at. The car is not raised at one end as such cars usually are, and as you hang on for dear life you are allowed to feel the full force of gravity, principally in the back of your neck. Oddly enough, as you look out of the windows you have the impression that you yourself are on a level and that Hong-Kong and the Peak are sliding into the sea. It is a singular illusion.

One Sunday night we walked down at dusk. Lights were beginning to twinkle in the harbor and a great yellow moon hung in the sky just above the horizon. The bells were ringing in the cathedral. The city looked gray and peaceful, and it seemed like Sunday to us for the first time since we left America. At night the hundreds of lights in the harbor are so starry that you might think a bit of the sky had fallen down to earth. The island of Hong-Kong is entirely a British possession, and the real name of the city is Victoria. There is a bronze statue of the queen in one of the squares, and I'm told that the Chinese all think she is as black as the statue is.

Of society there is plenty. Girls who like to cut a wide swath ought to come out to China, for they will have enough flattery and attention to turn their heads. Susceptible bachelors have a hard time of it, for the girls are all popular. It may be that after a while that worm in the bud, satiety, will creep in and rob Hong-Kong of some of its charm, but for a time it is fascinating and there are certainly many charming people who sojourn here. They do not call it "home," I observe. Home is England, or the States, or France, or Italy, or Spain—never Hong-Kong. The men-of-war and cruisers that are often in port do much to make it lively. The U. S. S. "Machias" has been here, and goes to-morrow to Canton. She has been dubbed "the matchbox" on account of her diminutive proportions, but she made a big noise with her salute to an admiral, a commodore, and the port the morning she arrived, and the papers complimented her on the rapidity with which the guns were fired.

One day we took tiffin with Admiral Monasterio of the Mexican navy on board the "Zaragoza," and came away with buttons and hat bands to our heart's content, beside the recollections of an unusually pleasant afternoon. The fad for collections grows and nothing seems to escape. We are beset by stamp dealers on every hand, and the value that those valueless bits of paper have grown to have is marvelous.

Everybody goes to Canton, and you can hear almost

In the China Sea

as many different opinions of it as there are people to give them. "Don't go! Horrible! Fascinating! Interesting! One day is more than you want! You can't see the place in a week!" and so on. As usual, the best way is to go and see for one's self. To describe it is quite another thing. One reads of the teeming millions in China and of the crowded cities, but nothing can paint the reality. Canton is seven or eight hours' ride from Hong-Kong by boat up the Pearl river. It is a very yellowish pearl that the river resembles, if any, and around Canton the water has the appearance and consistency of rich and creamy julienne soup. It is a pretty ride, between the low green banks of the broad river, while beyond lies the line of gaunt hills with which China seems to be everywhere guarded. The river sights are varied and interesting. There are the familiar junks and sampans of Shanghai and Hong-Kong, and beside, an odd little boat shaped like a pointed slipper, which skates around over the water like a water bug, leaving the same straight trail behind it. They travel wonderfully fast. Another curious craft is a large unwieldy passenger boat, patronized exclusively by Chinese and run by coolie power. There is a sort of treadmill in the stern, and you can see the naked coolies straining every muscle as they laboriously push the wheel.

XIV

In Canton

THE river life at Canton is a wonder. The number of souls who are born and live and marry and die on board the little sampans that jam the river is not known, but it is estimated in the hundreds of thousands. There is a social barrier—if I may use so dignified a term in connection with such a degraded lot of human beings—between the land and the river people, and they do not associate or intermarry. The sampans are only as long as a good sized row boat, and how families live on them is a mystery. Once I saw a little Chinese girl with a baby on her back fall into the water, and when she and the baby had been pulled on board, apparently no worse for their ducking, she was slapped for her carelessness.

One of the night sights of Canton is the gorgeously decorated "flower boats," where Chinese mandarins and the gilded youth go for amusement. The boats are flat-bottomed and give space for a good sized room which is decorated brilliantly with red and tinsel hangings and cushions. After the trip down the dark river from the hotel in a sampan with weird lights and crafts looming suddenly before one, the flower boats seem blazing with light and color. They are anchored side

SAMPANS AT CANTON

In Canton

by side and you can walk for a long distance on them if you have a care not to fall between. There is plenty of Chinese music and many gayly dressed Chinese men and women. Some of them are smoking opium, some tobacco, many drinking, but there is no disorder and they seem to take their larks rather seriously. We were escorted thither by "Susan," one of the characters of Canton. She was a poor little waif in whom some missionaries took an interest, and she developed great business ability, so great that she now owns several sampans and is much respected. A small urchin who displayed great executive ability in assisting us from one boat to another was pointed out as one of Susan's sons.

Ah Cum, Sr., and Ah Cum, Jr., were our guides and piloted us skillfully through the maze of streets of the city.

All the foreigners in Canton live on the island of Shameen, which is only reached by bridges and is guarded by detachments of soldiers in flowing red jackets decorated with black hieroglyphics. The Chinese, by the way, consider fighting degrading and have no respect for their soldiers. At night the gates of the bridges are all locked and no one is allowed to pass. This is done for the safety of the foreigners, and at times they have been in great danger there. "Foreign devils," the Chinese call us, and the great mass of them do not know that a white man exists. Some of them have become enlightened, our late notable guest, Li Hung Chang, for instance, but what a very little could a thousand Li Hung Changs do in a lifetime to move the dead weight of superstition, prejudice and ignorance that hangs over four hundred millions of people!

But Canton! Can you imagine miles upon miles of narrow, dark, dirty streets, winding and tortuous, where the dismal gray walls almost press against one another, so closely are they crowded? Well, adorn the walls with a quantity of multi-colored bills, then imagine a perfect shower of mysterious long, narrow signboards hanging in the air, through which few rays of sunlight manage to creep. Crowd and jam these passageways with pig-tailed men and moon-faced women and roly poly youngsters with goblin ears on their caps, add dogs, and chickens, and pigs, and smells to the collection, and you'll have an idea of Canton. I don't think there is a street more than eight feet wide in the city. They are paved with slippery, damp flagstones that have a habit of tipping up treacherously at one end when one steps on the other. Horses are almost unknown, I should say altogether unknown if I hadn't seen one official, evidently of highest importance, riding a poor little scrub of a white pony who looked as if he had seen much better days. Loads are all carried on coolies' shoulders, balanced and hanging from a bamboo pole. It is a marvel to everyone how the sedan chairs are ever forced through the crowds. The whole day there is one series of shouts and execrations from your coolies, and at night they ring in your ears in your dreams. They seemed to me to shout "So long!" but no doubt that was a mistake. If a man who is in the way doesn't make haste to get out they do not hesitate

In Canton

to assist him, and that not gently. One's nerves are apt to be worn to a raveling over the many narrow escapes from collisions and falls. Sometimes the passage of the chairs will block the street for a long distance. I say so much about this that you may have an idea of that first and most lasting impression of the crowded population. The beauty of living isn't studied in China.

I remember I wrote feelingly of smells in my last letter. Cologne is said to have seventy smells and none of them cologne, but I don't think seven thousand would cover the large and flourishing family of them in Canton. Kind Mr. da Cruz, the Portuguese proprietor of the Shameen hotel, thoughtfully provided us with a bottle of Wood Violets, for which we at various times blessed his name. The smells of the streets are bad enough, but the worst stenches come from the foul canals, of which there are many, filled with unmentionable abominations and reeking with filth.

There are high lights in this truly Rembrandtish picture, for in spite of its drawbacks I managed to report Canton as "well worth seeing." The streets are a panorama that is always unfolding, curious and interesting and varied. The shops are open and are usually lighted from the street, badly lighted goes without saying. There is the quarter of the fan dealers, the silk merchants, the shoemakers, the jade and the firecracker sellers, the pawnbrokers, the second-hand stores and many gambling establishments, for the Chinese are inveterate gamblers. Mixed in with these are the shops where eatables are sold. The vegetables look inviting enough and they have a fashion of arranging their wares in patterns which gives an air of neatness to the place but I couldn't possibly describe to you the messes of hideousness that are sold and eaten. Their greasy cakes are fried in grease that seems to have been in use since the time of Confucius. The fowls and animals in the meat markets are cleaned, and dried in conventional patterns by means of small sticks that push them out flat, then they are hung up by the tail, if they had one in life, or by a leg if they hadn't. We saw cats and dogs galore and many a string of flattened rats. I suppose you can have rat cutlets in the restaurants, and I know I took the precaution to order neither hash nor sausage at the hotel. We tried the Canton preserved ginger, though, and found it very good.

The beautifully embroidered Canton crepe shawls, that the Wise One says used to be the acme of elegance when she was a girl, are to be found in quantities in the silk shops. I managed to escape without one, though the fascination of buying was strong upon me, but, away from the temptation, I am now sure that I would much rather have something more modish with the cachet of Paris. There is an art in buying as there is in everything else, and at the last one is apt to feel that he has bought everything he did not want and nothing that he did. The beautifully embroidered Chinese garments have been a continual pitfall for us. When it is cold the people put on successive layers of clothes and some of the babies are so bundled up that I'm sure they couldn't touch the back of their necks with their hands.

In Canton

The children are cunning little youngsters and all as like as two peas. Indeed, for that matter, so are their elders. It has always been a matter of surprise to me how people manage to be so different, with two eyes and a nose and a mouth. The Chinese don't seem to succeed as well as we. It is with the greatest difficulty that I remember a face, for there is always that same expanse of yellow countenance, lighted by the same beady black eyes, with the same dangling queue. I believe there is a difference but it is hard to detect. The Eurasians, as the mixed Chinese and European blood are called, have a fascination for me. There is a fine looking young fellow whom I often see in the Hong-Kong hotel. He wears the Chinese costume, and from under his round black cap, with the red button on top, there descends a queue, but his skin is scarcely yellowish and his features and profile are absolutely Gibsonesque. A few of the Chinese wear spectacles, and they are always great circles of tortoise shell and glass that make their wearers look like owls. And have I told you that a soaring poet once referred to the Chinese women's feet as "golden lilies!"

The regulation sights of Canton are less interesting than the streets, but they afford a grateful rest from the eternal hubbub in the streets and are worthy of mention. No doubt they are worthy of study, too, and it has been observed that the longer a person lives out there the less he is inclined to give positive information on China and the Chinese. I'm told that in the interior many of the Chinese do not know that there has been a war with

One Way Round the World

Japan. Trade can not be carried inland because of the pirates that infest the navigable rivers and the natives tear up a railroad track as a "bad joss."

Pirates are always beheaded when convicted, and there is often an opportunity, for those who want it, to witness one of their grisly executions. Visitors are always taken to the execution ground in Canton. It is a long narrow strip of land near by a pottery, and when we saw it it was filled with clay jars that were drying in the sun. We did not have the experience of some of our friends who were ushered without warning into the place to find a dozen headless bodies and as many heads lying around on the ground. The men kneel in a line with arms folded and heads bowed awaiting their turn. Meanwhile they can watch the execution of those who come before them! I suppose they suffer very little in anticipation, however, for they are stoics and have absolutely no nerves. There are diabolical tortures, too, compared with which the execution is humane—crosses to which victims are fastened and cut in pieces, cages in which they can not get out of a cramped position and are left to die. Prisoners are taken around with a heavy board fastened around their necks, and at the court of justice one of our party saw a prisoner unmercifully flogged with a bamboo stick. "Bamboo chow chow," it is facetiously called. It may be that these modes of punishment are suited to the race and act wholesomely for the suppression of crime, but they are horrible.

A pleasant place to raise one's spirits, after such sights, is the Viceroy's garden, where Chinese capitalists

In Canton

and Americans can afford the rather modest sum that entertainment costs. The czar of Russia, who was then the czarovitch, lunched there when he was in Canton. It is a pretty garden with green clumps of bamboo and banana plants and beautiful bushes of the decorative scarlet poinsettia which grows luxuriantly here. There is a little lake in it and the effect is very summery and lovely. Other places that visitors see are the Five Storied and the Flower Pagodas. In another place there are 503 gilded images of Buddhist saints, including Marco Polo, who looks very foolish in a soft felt hat. All the saints have very long bulbous ears to show that they lived to an honorable old age.

The vaults where the rich lie in state before they are buried are interesting places. They are gay with lanterns and flowers and at a sort of shrine before the coffin there is a cup of tea and refreshments for the dead person. At one side there is a washbowl. The coffins are huge affairs made of logs and are said to be very expensive. One of them, a lacquered one, in which a Viceroy's wife lies, is said to have cost $6,000. She died from fright during the bombardment of Foo Chow.

At another place there is a primitive water clock in which the flight of time is registered by the dropping of water. All sight-seeing is unsatisfactory for it is dangerous to stop long enough to let a crowd gather around you.

XV

From Hong-Kong to Singapore

HONG-KONG was interesting to the last, and we came away with pleasantest memories of it. I like best to close my eyes and see the city as it looked at night from the bay. One evening when we were over at Kow Loon, just opposite Hong-Kong, we saw our old friend, the "Doric," which we had left in Yokohama, coming steaming up the stream. She was not expected until the next morning; in fact, she had broken the record from Shanghai to Hong-Kong, making the trip in fifty hours and some minutes. We hurried back to our launch, and steaming out to her, we climbed on board hardly five minutes after her engines stopped beating. I always find myself choosing words which apply to human beings when I'm talking of ships, for there is something so very human about their mechanical life. Their build carries out the idea, too, for they are tall and short, slender and stout, bustling and stately, just as people are.

The Doric and her crew were decidedly old friends, but there was a crowd of strange passengers aboard who didn't seem to belong there at all and with whom I was inclined to find fault.

It had grown dark and we leaned against the rail looking down at the jam of sampans below us pressing

From Hong-Kong to Singapore

against the ship's dark side, filled with anxious-faced Celestials who were shouting their fare to the Chinese passengers on board and on the alert for a customer. They all carried glowing lanterns, decorated with red characters. Beyond, the black water stretched away from us, and looking around we found we were hemmed in by a trail of starry lights which began at Kow Loon, were carried across the stream by the lights of the vessels and finished in a burst of scintillating fire in Hong-Kong itself. Up and down the hillside the lights hung in twinkling strands. It was as pretty as a carnival in Venice.

Another memorable evening was the evening of the governor's ball. It was given by the governor of the colony at Government House, a beautiful mansion, and all Hong-Kong's four hundred were there. The ball was the prettiest I've ever seen. The ball-room itself is imposing and the gowns of the women were beautiful; but the unusual and distinctive touch was the scarlet coats of the English officers. Every other man, at least, was in dress uniform, and the coats, though rather ludicrous as to cut, when examined singly, are brilliant in combined effect.

We sailed from Hong-Kong for Singapore on the Sunda, an intermediate steamer of the Peninsular and Oriental line. The intermediate steamers do not carry the mail but make about the same time that the mail steamers do, and are quite as comfortable. The first-class passengers were mostly English officers on their way home or in charge of the troops we had on board, and very agreeable gentlemen they were. Big Captain Sterling, aide-de-camp to the governor of Hong-Kong, whose acquaintance I made at the ball and renewed on the Sunda, is six feet four and three-quarters tall. As he walked along the decks he was in danger of knocking the life-boats overboard with his head. His proportions paled, however, beside those of a Singapore man whose height is six feet nine. I didn't see him, but he is well-known there, and his height is vouched for.

The Sunda gave us plenty of impressions of Tommy Atkins. Tommy Atkins, you know, is the name given to every British soldier. He got it from a blank form which was once sent through all the army to be filled out by the soldiers. A specimen one was made out and it began, "I, Thomas Atkins, do solemnly swear, etc." So the name was coined and it has stuck to the soldiers ever since.

There is more than one evidence of old England's sagacity in the far East. It begins with the safe pathway she has so wisely established from one end of her dominions to the other, starting with Gibraltar and ending at Hong-Kong. Her dominant influence is shown in the fact that you can speak English all the way around the globe, while in the East any other European language is rarely heard and almost unknown. All of her merchant vessels are prepared to carry troops on short notice, and England will never be caught napping. There were accommodations for a thousand men on the Sunda. In the harbor at Singapore there was a vessel floating

From Hong-Kong to Singapore

the Spanish flag. It was the old Atlantic liner Alaska, now turned into a transport ship carrying troops to Manila. We looked at her through a telescope and could see the soldiers swarming on her decks as thick as flies. She was carrying three thousand men, with proper accommodations for about a thousand, and she was in quarantine, having measles, smallpox and typhoid fever aboard. Her flag was always flying at half-mast, alas! for there were frequent deaths.

It is the opinion out here that Spain is making her "last kick" for her colonies. Every ship has brought younger and younger recruits, and these last are mere boys. The news from Manila is as horrifying as that from Cuba, and executions go on merrily at the rate of three or four a day. A well-known young Hong-Kong doctor was shot there a week or two ago for conspiracy in the rebellion, and two hours before the execution he was married to the girl he loved. There are two sides to the question of Spain's giving up her colonies, and one doesn't know where to place one's sympathies.

My remarks on Tommy Atkins seem to have died an early death as well as some of the patriots, and I think I'll not return to the subject, for my most vivid recollections of his presence are an irritating bugle that blew at all hours of the day and night and an unsavory odor of onions that was very often wafted over to us from his side of the ship and nearly sent us to the rail. He wasn't allowed to go on shore at Singapore, poor fellow, for he's apt to enjoy himself so much that he forgets to come back to the ship at all.

One Way Round the World

Would you enjoy just here a story of an old Scotchman which is not *"mal à propos?"* One evening the canny old gentleman was spending the evening with a party of convivial friends and about 9 o'clock he arose and began walking around solemnly to each of the party and saying good-night. "Why, Sandy!" they cried, "you're not going, are you?" "No," said he, "but I tho't I'd say gudenight while I still ken ye."

Even the bad sailors made the journey from Hong-Kong to Singapore without quiver or qualm. But such January weather! I suppose we shouldn't look for frost in the neighborhood of the equator, but I haven't a Spartan spirit, and I like to grumble about the heat. We sat on deck all day with awnings to shelter us from the burning tropical sun while drops of perspiration trickled down behind our ears and along our spinal columns. We tried to get in the path of the faint, hot breeze and lay in our steamer chairs watching the glassy water lazily dimpling instead of rippling—too lifeless to do anything but breathe. Down in the dining salon the punkahs made the air endurable, but the cabins were stifling. In the evenings the moon was so fine that there was rarely any of the evening left and sometimes some of the morning gone before we could make up our minds to go to bed. The punkah is a sort of long fan hung above the tables, and swung by a servant, which is much used in the East.

The native of Singapore considers a bit of drapery, a brilliant turban and a silver ring around his ankle, and it may be his toe, ample costume for a hot climate.

AN ORIENTAL COSTUME

From Hong-Kong to Singapore

Perhaps he's right. The heat is intense and yet this is the season of the year by courtesy called winter. The thermometer is not so high, but the humidity of the air makes the heat very oppressive. It rains almost every day of the year, and between sun and shower the most unwilling plant must grow and flourish. The bungalows, as the houses are called, stand in bowers of green. Even grim poverty is relieved by the lavish hand of nature, who weaves her garlands of verdure as carefully around the huts of the poor as the homes of the rich.

The native is a fortunate fellow. Like a true child of the tropics, he is lazy and shiftless, but discontent can not be counted among his faults. Pater familias has no harassing thoughts of Easter bonnets to torment him, neither does he need to take much thought for the raiment of himself or his family. A scrap of cloth without stitch or seam is all that is required for the older ones, and the little boys and girls omit costumes altogether. Fruits and nourishing nuts are to be had for the seeking, and there is always some warm and sufficiently comfortable place to lay his head. What wonder that he works only when he is driven to it.

The business of the place is almost entirely in the hands of the Chinese, but in the stream of humanity that swirls and eddies and then flows on through the strait almost every nation of the globe is represented. The resident community, too, is very cosmopolitan and includes almost all the nations of the East. There are Singhalese and Javanese, Indians, Chinese, Klings from the Madras coast, Japanese, men from Borneo, wild, for all I know, New Zealanders, Burmese, Siamese, all castes of Hindoos, Chetties, and many more. The intermarriage of the races and the mixture of blood adds to the confusion of the new-comers, and I'm sure it would be a long time before I could recognize them all readily. Their color varies from a yellowish cinnamon to **ebony**. The familiar riksha is one of the means of locomotion, but the **favorite is** a queer little bus called a gharry, drawn by a diminutive pony who is as **tough as a pine knot** and trots along with his heavy load at a brisk pace. Raffle's Hotel, named for the illustrious Raffle who **founded** the colony, **is a** lovely place with wide, cool verandas and many windowed rooms which look out on a luxuriant green garden filled with flowering shrubs and decorative palms. The Botanical Garden, too, is a place which everybody goes to see. It is a rarely lovely garden but a bit disappointing to me because it looked in many places much like our parks at home, and I had expected something strange. The jungle with its **wilderness of wild creeping things is much more beautiful.** Tigers still **roam there.** They swim over from **the** mainland **to the island** and occasionally the Sultan **of Johore gives a tiger hunt** which is of great interest to sportsmen. It is said that a native is eaten by a tiger on an average **every day in the** year, but that is probably an exaggeration.

The Chetties are interesting figures of Singapore streets. They come from India and are a rich and influential caste of money-lenders. There was a time when their word was as good as their bond, and in case of a failure the obligations of one were met by the others, but in the last few years some losses have been too heavy for them and they have lost the prestige they had. They are tall, dark, powerful fellows, scantily clothed in white. They shave their heads and around their necks they wear a massive ornament of pure gold. On their foreheads between their eyes they put a sticky substance which dries in a hard, round white wafer. I'm always thinking what capital ghosts they would make on a dark night, with only wafer, teeth, eyeballs and winding sheet in evidence.

It was our good fortune to see a procession which takes place annually when the god of silver is taken out for an airing and worshiped with many barbaric rites. We drove in a gharry from the hotel to the native part of the city where there is a Hindoo temple. The streets were full of picturesque figures in gay-hued clothes, bent on merry-making, apparently, more than worship, as holiday crowds are apt to be. We thought the Indian women with their lips and noses and ears pierced with silver and gold ornaments the most interesting. There were not many of them and the crowd was made up principally of men and children. Very few women are seen in the streets of Singapore, for the people have the Oriental idea of secluding them. I am speaking of the Oriental population, of course. There is a large English population, and some parts of the city are as English as England.

The little brown youngsters were a never-failing source

of amusement to us and the head of the family used up a roll of film on snap-shots.

At the end of the street where we entered we could see a gorgeous tinsel arch that seemed to be resting on the shoulders of a man, but he was so closely surrounded by the crowd that we could not get near enough to see him. If we stopped for a moment they crowded around us, and knowing that both cholera and small-pox were prevalent in Singapore, we didn't care to rub elbows with them. The man was evidently dancing, for the arch swayed and spun around and there was a jingling of bells. Afterward in the temple we saw a procession of dancers carrying the same gaudy arches and whirling in their frenzied dance. It was our first glimpse of barbarism, a revolting picture at which we gazed spellbound. The men were bare to the waist and their mouths and noses and ears were thrust through with long silver pins which were wet with blood. Their arms and chests and backs were literally full of shorter silver pins which had been thrust so deep into the skin that they stuck and hung there like a bristling coat of mail. The men were staggering and half fainting from exhaustion and some were supported by a couple of attendants who prevented them from falling as they tottered on in frenzied gyrations. The worshipers in the tawdry temple gazed at them unconcernedly. Our gharry man brought us some of the sticky, whitish paste so that we might put a wafer on our foreheads. It was decidedly gray with dirt and we rather reluctantly adorned ourselves to oblige him. He didn't know

BY JINRIKISHA IN SINGAPORE

From Hong-Kong to Singapore

enough English to explain the significance of it, but I afterward learned that the Hindoo decorates himself with the paste after his daily devotional ablutions and the style of adornment indicates his caste. There are hundreds of these castes in India and their complicated distinctions have presented the greatest difficulty to the authorities who are trying to stamp out the plague in Bombay. There would be riot instantly if the laws of caste were disregarded.

News of the plague's ravages reaches us every day, and we shall probably have to change our route in India and avoid the stricken city. There would be no great danger in going through Bombay, for the deaths from the plague are almost without exception confined to the natives, but all of the ports as far as Malta in the Mediterranean are quarantined against Bombay, and, as we should have endless difficulties on that account, it will be better to avoid it altogether.

.   .   .   .

Just a word about Penang, the most indescribable and the loveliest of all places we have seen. Other places have been tropical and beautiful but it is in Penang that nature's glories are most happily grouped and massed. There is a wealth of verdure and a wealth of bloom that carpets the rich red soil in wondrous harmony of colors, and above it all rise grove after grove of regal plumy cocoanut palms that wave so far above one's head that they seem to brush the blue sky. It is unsafe to call any place the most beautiful in the world, for you are sure to see something later that you like better and have to retract your rhapsodies, but I am tempted when I tell you of Penang.

We were delightfully entertained there by Mr. Jago, who has a lovely home and an interesting collection of rare orchids and ferns. The feathery fareleyensa, an exotic fern suggesting our maidenhair, grows to perfection in Mr. Jago's conservatories, in heavy clusters of richly shaded, exquisitely tinted green. The orchids too are wonderful, those rich radiant blossoms that seem the flower children of Mystery and Fascination. Perhaps, as Crawford thinks, they are like the soul.

It was in Penang that I had my first and last taste of a durian. The durian has a prickly green surface and looks like a huge chestnut burr. It smells, as somebody wittily said, like low tide. The taste is fearful. Imagine, if you can, a combined flavor of garlic, kerosene, asafetida and axle grease, and you have the aroma and the flavor of it. Yet people cultivate a taste for it and call it delicious. The mangosteen is another fruit of the Malay Peninsula, and it is truly delicious. The hard purplish outer shell is broken away, leaving a white center that is sweet, with a delicate touch of acidity, and has a flavor fit for the gods. However, I would change one this minute for a good rosy-cheeked Indiana apple.

I think it was Byron whose fancy was so airy and capricious that he never could love a woman after he saw her eat. It is a pity that eating is so popular, but in traveling, as elsewhere, one's comfort and happiness hinge on the first principles of good things to eat and good beds to sleep on.

WOMAN OF CEYLON

XVI

The Land of Gems and Flowers

PEERLESS Ceylon! Sunny land of flowers and fragrance, majestic forests and sparkling gems. She herself is like a radiant jewel lying on the bosom of the pulsing sea.

. . . .

From this poetic flight you will observe that I have been duly impressed by the charms which writers have tried in vain to describe and of which poets have vainly sung. Who can find adjectives that glow as color does, or verbs that smell sweet of spice, or nouns that burn like tropical skies? It is consoling to remember that we all have our limitations. As the composer of the immortal Boom-de-ay feelingly sang.

> " Shakespeare could write a play-ay
> But he never saw the day-ay
> That he could write Ta ra ra Boom-de-ay."

Perhaps James Lane Allen could paint as faithful a word picture of the jungle as he has of Kentucky woods and make one feel the quiver of heat in the tremulous air as he does the sharp touch of frost. I think of no other writer whose books are so full of atmosphere, as we might say of a painting.

One Way Round the World

Colombo is citified and fantastic, with as near an approach to bustle as the lazy Oriental is capable of producing. We were pleasantly introduced by being carried ashore in a "jolly" boat, and tarried awhile in the custom-house before going to the Grand Oriental. Calls and customs are inflictions from which the traveler to the ends of the earth probably does not escape. The Grand Oriental is a big, busy hotel that suggests the Grand at Yokohama, and has the same miscellaneous collection of foreigners under its roof.

It has a cosy, wide veranda fitted up with wicker chairs and tables, where people sit and drink and smoke, watching the passers-by in the street or bargaining with the insistent vendors of lace and jewelry and pudgy ebony and ivory elephants, who swarm around like flies. Colombo is supposed to be a great market for gems, particularly sapphires, but to begin with, they are badly set and then the best of everything is picked up by the expert European and American buyers. The dealers are a set of the most artistic liars that I have ever met. I thought the unprincipled scallawags who keep the little shops along the Tiber in Rome the most perfect specimens of their kind in existence, but I hadn't been to Ceylon. The streets are lined with little jewelry shops all displaying very much the same line of wares, and I've never heard of any one who succeeded in walking along the sidewalk without being pulled into some of them. The dealers have no hesitation about selling for what they can get, and they unblushingly accept a half or a quarter or a fifth of the price that they ask for

A "JOLLY" BOAT

an article. There may be some reliable men among them, but I fear Diogenes would get out his lantern. If you are a judge, well and good, for the dealer soon finds that out and bargains accordingly, but if you are uninformed, as most people are, beware! I asked a resident of Colombo whether there was a shop where a person who was not a judge of stones could be sure of being asked a reasonable price and he replied, "I'm afraid not." Moonstones are plentiful and cheap; there are also many cat's-eyes that have the elusive charm of the opal, rings upon rings of sapphires and pearls and rubies, set principally in gypsy fashion. For the lovers of the curious there are many quaint bits of old Singhalese jewelry, combs and rings and necklaces. I have in my mind an odd barbaric ring set with all the jewels of Ceylon, and a unique necklace of strings of seed pearls separated by carnelian balls overlaid with a delicate network of gold.

Gambling is said to be as great a curse to the Singhalese as to the Chinese. Sometimes you see the coolies squatting beside their rikshas, watching something very intently. They have put a couple of silver coins on the shafts of the vehicle and are waiting to see on which a fly will alight first. The dealer has the same spirit. He will toss, if you like, for a jewel for which he asks ten rupees. "Master toss, twenty rupees or nothing."

The streets are filled with the same motley crowd as in Singapore, though there are few Chinese. There are a good many Moors in Colombo. They wear queer variegated silk hats, woven like straw, that look like inverted waste paper baskets, and a long white coat that appears to be an evolution of the Prince Albert. There are many families from Southern India, darker and more barbaric than the regular-featured, intelligent-looking Singhalese. The Kling laborers are figures that would make Indianapolitans open their eyes if set down in Washington street. As in Singapore, they consider a bit of drapery and a brilliant turban ample costume for a hot climate and a general absence of superfluity in clothing is noticeable. The Tamils make up for the deficiency by a quantity of nose and ear ornaments, bracelets and anklets. I send a picture of a little Tamil bride, ten years old. The piece just above the necklace with the three hanging amulets shows that she is a married woman. Her father is a very rich man and her ornaments are all gold. Her dress is silk but with the Oriental disregard of detail her skirt is tied on with a piece of jute string. The Tamil women cut great pieces out of the lobes of their ears and weight them down with heavy ornaments.

The Singhalese girls are very pretty. They have large, soft eyes, good features and round, shapely figures. They wear odd little low-necked white jackets usually trimmed with crocheted lace, a fashion that I fancy was introduced by the Dutch, a bright-colored skirt and few ornaments. Both men and women have a look of refinement and intelligence. The Singhalese men are very womanish in appearance. They have long curling black hair that is shiny with cocoanut oil

SNAKE CHARMER AND JUGGLER

and is done up in a knot at the back of their heads just as a woman's is. At the top of the head they wear a circular tortoise-shell comb. Of garments they have few. The real native costume is a yard or two of cloth; in the cities some of the men wear European coats but usually they have none. Large checks are still in vogue in Ceylon, worn skirt fashion and fastened on by a leather belt.

We used to entertain ourselves at the G. O. H., as the Grand Oriental is always called, by watching the performance of an Indian magician, who sits in front of the veranda. He has a vicious cobra that hisses and rears its flat head threateningly, and he plays a weird tune on a peculiar musical instrument which apparently charms the snake. As soon as a little crowd of idlers has gathered around him the magician shuts the cobra up in a basket and begins his performance. His tricks are not elaborate, but they are very skillfully done, quite enough so to be entertaining. The man squats on the ground not more than six or eight feet from his audience, and having no accessories in the way of lights and curtains, he has to be very expert to deceive. He does the mango trick, making the mango shrub grow from the seed in a few moments, very well indeed. It remained a mystery to all of us. However, the seed does its growing under a square of cloth, and that takes the edge off of a supernatural flavor that it might otherwise have. The tales of the miraculous performances of the far-famed East Indian jugglers are not well authenticated.

One Way Round the World

The residence part of Colombo is almost as lovely as that of Penang, and it has the same low red-roofed bungalows, surrounded by the same flowery gardens overhung by groves of the same graceful cocoanut palms. The native part of the city is dirty, with rows of squalid one-roomed houses, in which sometimes two or three families seem to be living. As a whole the place is disgusting, but that doesn't prevent one from coming occasionally upon very charming bits of life that delight snapshotters and are worthy of a frame and a place on a great gallery's walls—perhaps a dark Tamil beauty standing in an attitude of easy grace in a doorway and showing her white teeth in a smile, perhaps a handsome mother walking with an even swinging step and carrying a brown baby who sits astride her hip and wears some silver bracelets and anklets and a silver chain around his fat little waist for all his adornments, perhaps a shapely brown little boy with a red cap and bright eyes. The streets are full of top-heavy carts drawn by little bullocks who look ridiculously disproportionate to the vehicle and who are driven by a rope tied through their nostrils. They are slow but sure and are really not so heavily loaded as they appear. The carts have a high hooded rush cover that protects from the sun and rain and is, of course, very light. The passenger vehicles are little wagons called hackeries, also drawn by diminutive bullocks, and advancing at a rate well suited to the Singhalese temperament. I should have nervous prostration if I had to ride in them a mile; fortunately

A SINGHALESE GROUP

The Land of Gems and Flowers

there are jinrikishas and stout English horses for the stranger within the gates.

One evening we went for a drive along the Galle Face road. That distressing name seems to have been given to it because there is a peninsula beyond called Point de Galle. The place is heavenly. I use the world advisedly. The road skirts the sea and there is something singularly majestic and grand about the ocean there, as it rolls up on the glassy wet beach in curling, foaming, thundering white waves. It was sunset. There had just fallen one of those beating tropical rains that wash the sky clean and leave it clear and blue as a sapphire. The air was sweet and fresh, and the damp road, red when it is dry, was a rich maroon. To the right lay a level stretch of vivid green, dotted with the gay hued figures of natives and fringed at the horizon with palms. Toward the west the sea and sky were one blaze of burnished metallic opal tints. It seems as if wind and weather had the same impulsive disposition as the children of the tropics. Sun and shower follow one another in quick succession, and the rain is fierce while it lasts. The glory was quickly gone. The fiery tints melted into gray and the shadowy ships sailed away into the dusk.

That is what we all have—the glory of the skies. Perhaps it is the universal message.

. . . .

A punster would surely make material of the fact that Buddha's left eye-tooth rests in Kandy. I don't know the tooth's history, that is its early history, whether it was extracted in life or whether it was decorously presented after the great teacher's death. I must whisper, too, that the sacred tooth which is thought worthy of a temple to enshrine it and is an object of veneration to 400,000,000 people, is the subject of many an irreverent jest among unbelievers. It was lately exhibited in honor of some Siamese prince or other and somebody who saw it pronounced it the tooth of an alligator. If it corresponds with a foot-print of Buddha that I paid a few coppers to see, it should be about that size.

The Dalada Maligana or temple of the Sacred Tooth is in Kandy, and it is to Kandy we go from Colombo. The ride up into the mountains is an interesting and beautiful one. The slopes are covered with a strange and lovely vegetation and the types of natives are endless. Even the animals are curious, the little humpbacked bullocks and particularly the ugly gray buffaloes. Sometimes in a marshy place you will see what seem to be a lot of gray rocks along the surface of the water, but when you see some of the rocks move you discover that they are the noses and faces of a herd of buffaloes that have placidly waded as far as possible into the water both to keep cool and to avoid switching flies. Some writer on Ceylon referred to these animals as "the mud caressing buffalo," but in my mind I do not connect mud with caresses. The little bullocks, which are not amphibious, have their hides fancifully decorated with stripes and circles and scallops, the scars of cruel

NATIVE BUNGALOWS NEAR KANDY

The Land of Gems and Flowers

cuts that are made with a sharp knife when the bullock is young.

Kandy itself is delightful. The air is much cooler than in Colombo and the town encircles a pretty artificial lake made for the last Kandyan king and intended for his own private use. This district has a history of bloodshed, horrible cruelty and long warfare with Portuguese, Dutch and English invaders, but it is at last peaceably in the hands of the English and the last Kandyan king has been gathered to his forefathers. Photographs will tell you the story of Kandy's loveliness. My instinct for photographs is becoming so developed that I find myself drawing a line around everything I see and imagining it on a plate. A drive around the lake takes one past many cozy bungalows with deep pillared verandas and luxuriant gardens. Many of them are filled with bushes of poinsettia, flamboyant, as it is well named out here. Its gorgeous wheels of scarlet and gold are a favorite resting place for the gauzy winged flies and brilliant butterflies. By moonlight the bold fronds of the palms stand out in black relief against the sky. I look in vain for my old friends among the stars. They are either so changed in position that I can't recognize them or they have disappeared altogether beneath the rim of the horizon. One drawback to tropical loveliness is the large number of venomous creatures that live in the jungles. We have become accustomed to the lively little lizards that play tag on our bedroom walls and the giant beetles that bump clumsily around the room. Fortunately we haven't had any encounters with scorpions or centipedes, though they say that in some places you have to take care to shake your shoes in the morning before putting them on. "They say," however, is a sad prevaricator. Another drawback is the weekly return of our wrecked washing. The garments are washed by men who batter them against a rock until they are a delicate pearl gray and return them in tatters.

The Temple of the Tooth may be visited many times and always with fresh interest. It is not a beautiful place but very curious. The tooth, so a legend runs, was formerly at Danta-poora, near Calcutta. Many attempts were made by the Brahmins to destroy it by fire but it always reappeared folded in a lotus blossom. Elephants trod upon it, but it rose from the earth in a lotus of silver and gold. It was cast into sewers and the sewers were immediately transformed into beautiful lakes. Finally it was carried to Ceylon in the dusky tresses of an Indian princess and here it has remained ever since. Once a year, in August, there is a grand procession called the "Perahara," when the tooth is taken from the temple and carried through the streets on an elephant's back. It is rarely shown to anyone, but has been seen on the occasion of a visit of royalty. At that time the Kandyan chiefs appear in their robes of state. The robe of state in Kandy is a very complicated affair, indeed, and it is said there are a hundred and fifty yards of silk in it. Most of it is gathered in a great wad under the belt, and the Kandyan chief in full regalia must be a comical object. His mien is dignified

THE TEMPLE OF THE TOOTH

The Land of Gems and Flowers

but the little white ruffles around his ankles are not. Opposite the temple is a bell-shaped shrine, called a dagoba. These dagobas vary in size from small metal ones studded with jewels, which envelop relics, to buildings of gigantic size. The temple itself is enclosed by a wall and a moat filled with water in which the sacred tortoises are swimming.

Entering a small quadrangle one goes up a flight of steps into a sort of an anteroom to the inner shrine. Along the way there are some highly colored Egyptian-like frescoes that represent the torments in store for sinners—those who pluck the leaves of the sacred bo tree, those of a lower caste who insult those of a higher, and so on through a list of evil doing.

The sight in the anteroom is a memorable one. First you are conscious only of a terrific tomtoming that is fairly splitting your ears. Tomtoms are native drums much liked by the noise-loving Oriental, and the drummers in the temple whack them vigorously. The room is crowded with reverent worshipers wearing many rich colored fabrics, and occasionally a brown shaven priest draped in yellow passes by. The air is heavy with the fragrance of flowers which are being sold from booths at either side of the room. This is the pretty offering that the devout Buddhist offers at the shrine of the tooth. Only the corolla of the flower is used and bushels of them are piled up in fragrant confusion. They are renewed every morning so they are fresh and dewy. The fragrant plumiera with pure creamy petals and yellow heart, the jasmine and the oleander are favorites.

Passing through a doorway which has elephant's tusks on either side, and mounting a steep staircase you come to another door elaborately inlaid with silver and ivory. Passing through this door you are in the shrine. Inside an iron cage is a silver dagoba hung with jeweled ornaments, given by the last Kandyan king, who built the temple. Inside the large dagoba are seven smaller ones studded with precious stones, and under the last one rests the sacred tooth in the heart of a golden lotus.

It is all very barbaric and curious, and it is surprising to find in the library a priest who has been to England and speaks English admirably. He showed us some books written on narrow strips of palm leaf pierced with a hole at either end and tied between covers of massive silver. They are written with a stylus in the classic Pali language, and the priest wrote my name for me on a bit of palm leaf, in Singhalese characters. The palm is as useful as the bamboo and there is one variety, the Talipot, that is said to have 801 uses. It furnishes sunshades and rain coats, tents, fans, paper, and so on.

There is a stud of forty fine elephants kept by the temple for the Perahara procession. They are not as interesting as the big, sagacious fellows that one sees at work. These huge but gentle beasts do all kinds of heavy work, obeying a word from their masters though they could crush them with one blow. One morning we saw an elephant which was rolling a big log up a hill. We stopped to watch him and he brought it out

AN ELEPHANT AT WORK

The Land of Gems and Flowers

into the road, put it down, and at his master's suggestion came over and made a profound salaam to us. In the elephant corrals, as the catching of elephants is called, when they are not killed the tame elephants help to drive the wild elephants into an enclosure and afterward help to tame them. The jungles are full of leopards, tigers, elephants and monkeys, and all kinds of reptiles. The prettiest drive from Kandy is to the Peradeniya Garden. The road is one long vista of green and bloom, and by the roadside are the mud huts of the natives, thatched with palm leaves. There is a legend that the palm tree can not live far from the sea nor from the sound of human voices.

The natives tempt me to use again that overworked word picturesque. I like best the bright-eyed, brown little boys with their ready smile and gleaming rows of even, white teeth. They are Palmer Cox's brownies in the flesh. The cunning small children wear no clothing at all. Fortunately they are black. In the distance they caper like animated silhouettes and near by a stretch of the imagination turns them into little bronzes. The men's lips and teeth are blood red from chewing the betel nut. The women are very often seen carrying a round earthen water jar which rests on the hips. They all seem careless and contented. Dinner is growing at the door and work is irksome.

The spice trees of the beautiful Peradeniya Garden are perhaps the most interesting. It is novel to walk about picking up little bunches of green cloves that have just fallen from the tree, or nibbling at a green nutmeg or chewing a stick of fresh cut juicy cinnamon. The cinnamon odor carries farthest, and when it is being gathered the perfume is wafted miles and miles out to sea. You can pick a bit of cinchona bark from the tree or amuse yourself touching the sensitive plant that carpets the ground in many places. It is covered with starry, purplish blossoms and droops pathetically at the slightest touch. The India rubber is a stately tree with wonderful snaky roots that stand out of the ground and if bruised exude a whitish rubber. I bought a solid ball of the strings wound tight upon one another which bounces finely. The spreading banyan tree flourishes and sends its arms to the ground for support. A beautiful fan palm is known as the traveler's palm, because it holds about a quart of pure water at the base of each of its spreading leaves. The cocoa bushes are filled with the dark red cocoa pods. There is a curious candle tree with long green pods that look like candles hanging directly from the bark of the tree instead of from the branches. The jak fruit, big and green, but with the flavor of a potato, grows the same way.

The giant clump of bamboos is wonderful. This ambitious member of the grass family has stalks that are nine inches in diameter and a hundred feet high. In the rainy season if you hang your hat on a stalk of bamboo at night, you'll have to have a ladder to reach it in the morning.

The Mahawelliganga is a river that almost encircles the garden. Indian and Singhalese names leave nothing to be desired. In fact one would be satisfied with

GIANT BAMBOO

The Land of Gems and Flowers

less. This is a list of simple ones. Anuradhapura, Pollonarua, Henaratgoda, Nawalapitiya, Rambukkana, Kadugannawa.

Newara-Eliya, humanely shortened to "Nuralia" in pronunciation, is a mountain resort far above Kandy which is popular with Europeans, but is too much like our own mountain scenery to be well worth visiting. All the way from Kandy to Newara-Eliya the mountains are almost entirely covered with tea fields. It is the tea which is now being so widely advertised in the States, by the government, I'm told, for the benefit of the planters. Formerly all this tea land was in coffee, but a blight destroyed all the bushes. We saw the entire process of preparing tea for the market. It is a simple one of picking the tender leaves from the low tea bushes and rolling and drying them artificially. At last the leaves are sifted and sorted and sealed in lead foil ready for shipment.

. . . .

We leave for Calcutta by the Chusan, in spite of ominous reports of the plague and the danger of quarantine. The disease is still confined to Bombay and the danger of contagion is very slight.

XVII

What We Saw in India

WE were leaning idly against the rail of the Chusan as she lay in the harbor at Colombo.

"Hop-o-die! Hop-o-die!" called a row of black individuals who were sitting on their heels on a rude raft made of three logs of wood lashed together. They sat at equal distances from one another, as neatly arranged as peas in a pod, and each one paddled with a split section of a bamboo pole in lieu of an oar.

"Hop-o-die! Hop-o-die!" they called, looking anxiously at the people along the rail and evidently on the alert for something.

The Chusan was supposed to sail at 10 A. M. from Colombo, and there had been a vast hustle and bustle and confusion in the Grand Oriental Hotel to get her passengers off by that time. The very pulse of the port hotel is the arrival and departure of the ocean steamers. When they are in port everything is full of life and movement. Even the punkahs feel the current and flap vigorously. Then when the ships sail away again carrying their passengers on with them, or the passengers have departed for the sights in the interior, the hotel settles down into a calm which by contrast is desolate, to be revived in a short season by a new regiment of globe trotters. One of the pleasantest features of the long journey around the globe is the meeting and re-meeting of fellow-travelers who have been a steamer ahead of you or perhaps a steamer behind, and who finally cross your path again. But, as I was saying, the Chusan's passengers, after a deal of fuss and tribulation, arrived on board in peace and in a perspiration, at 10 o'clock. A last tempting bit of freight must have been at the bottom of it, for we didn't sail until 4 P. M. and were left to entertain ourselves, meanwhile, with the venders of moonstones and coarse hand-made lace, who clambered on board. Bargaining with the Oriental is an affair of time and patience and my disposition is being ruined by their methods. Besides, I am a jaded shopper by this time and it requires something rare or unusual to hold my attention. It was much more entertaining to lean against the rail and watch the craft that pressed against the ship's dark side. There were big cargo boats alongside, filled with boxes and bales that the dark-skinned coolies were hoisting on board. Then came the smaller passenger boats and a curious craft called an outrigger canoe or catamaran. The boat is a narrow coffin-shaped affair that stands high out of the water, and would instantly topple over if it were not held upright by a floating bar of wood that is fastened to the side of the canoe by a couple of arching arms. They look very ticklish and I should be afraid to wink one eye without the other if I were a passenger.

"Hop-o-die! Hop-o-die!" called the black urchins.

One Way Round the World

"What are they saying?" said I to my neighbor, who shall be known as the Gentleman from Madras.

"Don't you recognize your mother tongue?" he replied. "They want you to throw a coin and they are saying, 'Have a dive! Have a dive!'" Before we had time to find a small silver piece and throw it into the water the remarkable quintet arose from their sitting position and stood like a row of crows on their shaky raft. Their costume was microscopic and their expression one of deep solemnity. At a signal they began clicking their elbows sharply against their bare sides, marking time by the resounding slaps, and suddenly, without a word of warning, they burst into song. "Ta-ra-ra Boom-de-ay!" they howled, as solemn as owls, slapping themselves vigorously first on one side and then the other, and singing as if their lives depended on it, a garbled version of Lottie Collins's *chef-d'œuvre*. You may travel around the globe from pole to pole and I'm sure you'll find nothing more comical than the fervent rendition of "Ta-ra-ra" which those imps of darkness give. We were convulsed with laughter, and a shower of silver bits began to fall over the Chusan's side. As soon as a coin struck the water there was a lunge from the raft, five bodies darted through the air and in a tangle of brown legs the whole party disappeared under the water. In a moment they were up again and one of them would triumphantly display the shining silver coin. They are clever divers and will even dive under the ship for a consideration.

The devil dancers of Ceylon are a curious institution.

DEVIL DANCERS OF CEYLON

What We Saw in India

When anyone of means is very ill he sends for the devil dancers. They dress themselves in the most hair-raising costumes and dance around the dwelling, beating tom-toms and gongs. At a critical point in an illness such a racket usually causes a man to rally or kills him outright and the devil dancers have the reputation of effecting most wonderful cures. Probably the idea is the same as with the Chinese, that the noise frightens away the evil spirits that are flocking around to take the man's life.

We had a large and flourishing collection of Anglo-Indian babies on board the Chusan, pink-and-white wholesome-looking youngsters who were born in India and had been home to England for a visit. They trotted around the deck, followed by their Indian "ayahs," as their nurses are called, and made life alternately delightful and miserable for the passengers.

I talked often with the Gentleman from Madras. He was one of those cordial Britons who has lived for years in the East and is distinctly more agreeable than his countrymen at home. The Gentleman from Madras had India and its history at his tongue's end and was ever ready to tell some of his interesting experiences, perhaps of an exciting tiger hunt, perhaps of an audience with a rajah. He knew Col. Olcott, Annie Besant and Madame Blavatsky very well. "*De mortuis nil nisi bonum,*" he said of the latter. Col. Olcott, the apostle of theosophy, lives near Madras and his home is the Mecca of theosophists. I remember him very well, as I crossed the Atlantic with him several years ago, a big, genial man with snowy hair and beard which made him look like Kris Kringle, and I regret that our stay in Madras was too short to allow us to call and renew acquaintance with him.

On all the long eastern coast of India there is no natural harbor, and the artificial one at Madras was made at tremendous cost, a million tons of concrete blocks being used. At one time it was almost destroyed by a cyclone and the storm's fury can still be seen in the row of slanting undermined blocks that lie outside the new and firm walls. The surf is usually strong inside the harbor, and as there are no docks, the landing of passengers and freight is often tedious and even dangerous. The instability of human affairs is never more graphically realized than when one stands uncertainly on the lowest step of a ship ladder ready to get into a pitching, rocking small boat which first rises alluringly quite within reach of your foot and then sinks suddenly to a dizzy depth below it. We were fortunate in having a comparatively calm day, and as soon as our big ship sailed within the encircling arms of the harbor walls the native boats began to put out from the shore. The boats are high, open craft made of thin planks stitched with cocoanut fiber. They make me think of a section of a foot-ball. They were manned by a double dozen of rowers who pulled long oars made of a straight bar of wood with a round wafer attached to the end, which did duty as a blade.

Madras from a distance is imposing, the graceful domes of the law courts rising clear and beautiful against the sky. A closer inspection of Blacktown and Whitetown, as the native and European quarters are called, reveals little that is beautiful and much that is repulsive and dirty. The only charm is the brilliant, slow-moving, panorama of the streets. The Oriental saunters and idles, never jostling, never hurrying. If time flies he bids it godspeed, and goes on his way leisurely.

In Madras we rode on an electric car line, the only one in India, I believe. Its swift flight seems curiously out of place in the lazy streets, but at least it outwits the burning sun and furnishes a refreshing breeze.

The bullocks are even smaller than in Ceylon, and how the fat passengers squeeze into the little carts is a mystery. The little bullocks very often have one horn painted red and one green and they wear strings of beads around their necks. The religion of a Mussulman or Hindu does not permit him to take the life of an animal, but it doesn't prevent him from abusing one. The bullocks are meek, docile-looking creatures, but they are unmercifully thumped and whacked and pounded by the drivers, while their poor little tails are twisted into corkscrews. Perhaps they are like the wily mule and their mild mien gives no hint of their latent determination.

In one place we saw a great crowd assembled in an open square evidently waiting to see some one who was to come out of the temple near by. We thought of stopping and afterwards regretted that we did not, for we learned that the crowd was waiting to see Swami Vive Kananda, a noted Brahmin preacher whom the Wise One had met in Chicago. It was he who represented the Brahmo Somaj religion in the Parliament of Religions.

The last place to look for Madras plaids is in Madras. We spent a quite unwarranted length of time looking for some of the rich colored cotton fabrics which we call Madras plaids. Perhaps they are made in Manchester. It is a fact that a large number of gay blankets and plaids are woven in Manchester for the Indian trade. Even fabrics have their ups and downs. There is denim that used to shine in overalls, now enthroned as a high art textile.

A band of the cleverest jugglers that we have seen entertained us on board the steamer. They did dozens of the cleverest and most mysterious tricks, but by far the most remarkable was what is known as the basket trick. A woman is tied in a net and pushed into a basket which seems hardly large enough to contain her body. The basket stands on the deck surrounded by a ring of people and there is no chance of changing it in any way or substituting another one for it. After the cover is put on the man calls to the woman and a muffled voice from the basket answers. Then he takes a murderous looking long knife and thrusts it right and left through the basket, apparently in every direction, rapidly and fiercely. There are shudders and ohs and ahs from the mystified spectators. After a little while the cover is lifted and the woman gets out, free from the net which had been tied in stout knots around her, and unharmed. She is apparently wedged so tight in the basket that she has to be helped to free her head. It is a most wonderful illusion. The basket must be deceptive in size and yet there it is right under your eyes and not six feet away. How the woman ever manages to escape being pierced by the knife is marvelous. It goes clear through the basket and sticks out on the other side. There must be room for her to move and avoid it, and yet the basket doesn't shake and the knife is thrust through and through in quick succession. It is easy to understand how these adept jugglers get the reputation of having miraculous powers.

The Hooghly is one of the shower of streams that form the delta of the Ganges. You may spell it with variations, Hooghly, Hugli, Hoogli, Hughli, and defy any one to prove that your spelling is wrong. Hindustani coquets with the alphabet. There are half a dozen ways of spelling every Indian name, and this or that authority is sure to clash with your own ideas of the way the thing should be done. Probably the confusion arose when the Hindustani names first began to be used in English. It is likely that they were carelessly spelled as they sounded, without any rule of pronunciation. Jeypore, for instance, is, I believe, properly spelled Jaipur, but Jeypore is much more familiar.

As we neared Calcutta the question of the day's run and the pool thereon, which always furnishes a certain stir and excitement on board, was laid aside for the more engrossing topic of taking on a pilot. Here was a new field for speculation into which we all rushed eagerly. A pilot on shore is a commonplace individual enough, but when he comes on board a ship he is the hero of the hour. It was past midnight when we sighted a ghostly brig that was signalling to us with a flaring torch. We ran as near her as it was safe to do and our panting engines stopped, leaving us rocking like a cradle on the swelling waves. In a few moments we saw coming toward us a very speck of yellow light, a will o' the wisp that danced on the crest of a wave and then swiftly disappeared. The sea was glittering and glassy, and the powerful out-running tide pulled and tugged at the ship's side. Presently we could see that the yellow light was in a staunch little boat, and we watched its rowers fight inch by inch for their way as they came toward us. The water swished and curled and sucked, but the boat held its ground and gained steadily. At last it was alongside and the much heralded pilot clambered on board. The Hooghly is a shifting, treacherous stream, and its pilots are as skillful as any in the world. The Ganges is lower this year than it has been for thirty-three years, and the quicksands are more than usually dangerous. As we went up the river the men stood by the boats ready to lower them at an instant's warning. On our way we saw the masts of the City of Canterbury sticking out of the water. She sank a few weeks ago. The passengers were rescued, but lost all of their luggage. She was a fine, big ship, and the sight of the tips of her masts above the water, combined with the fact that the men on your own vessel are standing by the life boats, is apt to make you feel, as we used to say at boarding school, "vivid along your backbone."

We wound and twisted with the channel, almost

tying loops in our course, and when the dangerous part was passed we steamed steadily up the stream between green banks of plumy cocoanut palms and tangled jungle, where the sportsmen tell you there is rare tiger shooting.

Near the city are the ruins of the palace of the last king of Oude and many dismantled mansions in what was once the fashionable part of town.

At the dock we crawled down a particularly long, particularly slippery and particularly tilted gang-plank, in imminent danger of having our heads bumped by the trunks which the coolies were carrying down on their heads, and climbed into the least disreputable of a disreputable row of gharries that were waiting there.

The gharry is a ramshackle box of a carriage, drawn by two lean horses, steered by a lean driver and furnished with irritating sliding side doors that insist upon sliding in the direction that you do not want them to, whichever that may be. We watched our baggage piled in a shaky pyramid on another gharry, not without misgivings, and afterward made a note of another dodge adopted by the fertile heathen for extracting money, for the baggage might just as well have gone with us.

"At last we are on shore!" said the Wise One, as we rattled away, and we leaned back and sighed two sighs of relief. The Wise One's sighs of relief and my own are a continual source of edification to me. "At last we are on shore!" we exclaim rapturously at the end of a sea voyage. "At last we are at sea!" we cry exultantly after a journey overland.

One Way Round the World

There was formerly a shrine to the dread goddess Kali on the site of Calcutta, and from it the city is named. Kali is a hideous divinity, gory and bloodthirsty, who wears a necklace of human skulls. She sends pestilence and scourge and famine and is only appeased by blood. In former times human sacrifices were frequently made to her and even in late years, in time of famine and distress, human heads decked with flowers have been found before her shrines.

Calcutta, the city, is only of passing interest. It is neither flesh, nor fowl nor good red herring. Some one not inaptly called it the city of palaces and defective drains. Luxury walks side by side with misery.

I came to India hampered with very little knowledge of its history but I remembered the shivers that the Third Reader tale of the "Black Hole of Calcutta" used to give me and I looked up the spot. It is now covered by a modern and handsome post-office and the place is marked by a stone pavement about fifteen feet square, which lies in an entrance court. On an arched gateway is an inscription which tells that the stones near by mark the size and situation of the dungeon in the old fort known in history as the "Black Hole of Calcutta."

Government House is a noble mansion that stands in the usual well-groomed English garden. There the Viceroy of India lives in regal state during the short winter months, and in summer the whole government machinery is moved to Simla, in the hills. The Viceroy receives about $100,000 a year for his services and is appointed for five years.

What We Saw in India

Beyond the garden of Government House is the beautiful Maidan, Calcutta's pride and joy. It is a handsome wide, open green, hardly a park, crossed by drives and foot paths and dotted with fine shade trees. In the evening it is filled with fashionable people in smart turnouts with Indian servants in gorgeous livery. I liked it rather better at midday when the trees threw an inviting shade and the occasional brilliant figures of the natives stood out on the green sward like brilliant flowers. Very often we would see a faithful Mohammedan bowing low at his prayers with his face turned toward Mecca. It is the month of Ramizan and Mohammedans eat nothing from sunrise to sunset. It rather spoils the effect of their piety to know that they eat all night. The beautiful Chowringhi Road with its row of handsome clubs and dwellings, and its museum building faces the Maidan.

The business houses of the East are as different from our own as they well could be. Sometimes they stand in decorous rows as they do at home, especially in the large cities, but very often you will drive to the banker's or the druggist's or the photographer's, enter a gateway by a shady drive and find a flower garden in front of the home-like building.

XVIII

A Glimpse of the Ganges

WE have had rather a surfeit of zoological and botanical gardens and have grown painfully unenthusiastic over rare fauna and flora, but we were still charmed by the gardens in Calcutta. In the zoological garden there are some splendid tigers, huge, tawny, beautifully striped fellows, and all the animals were fine specimens of their kind. The birds, too, were rarely beautiful; dainty little songsters in coats of many colors, gorgeous birds of paradise, with all the tints of sunset in their wings, exquisite gray cockatoos with soft pinkish breasts and creamy white crests, flaming parrots, resplendent peacocks, with blue-green glistening throats—all the feathered beauties of the tropics.

The Botanical Garden is beautifully laid out and filled with glassy pools that reflect the rich foliage of bamboos and palms and plantains on their banks. The glory of the garden is a wonderful banyan that is a forest in itself. It is a hundred and twenty-five years old, and the main trunk has a circumference of fifty feet, five and a half feet from the ground. At the crown this grand old giant has a circumference of nine hundred and twenty feet. Its wide spreading branches are up-

A Glimpse of the Ganges

held by no less than three **hundred and** seventy-eight aerial roots. Some of them **have grown as** thick as the trunks of a large tree. The banyan's branches spread widely, and **as** they grow send **down at intervals tufts** of hairy strands that finally reach **the ground and take** root, eventually supporting the branch **as it** grows longer. The banyan at Calcutta is monarch of them all, the largest in the world, and from a distance it is **a** great mound of verdure. When one is underneath it **is** a fairy bower of green through which the sunlight **falls in** quivering flakes of gold. The garden is filled **with** creepers that run riot on the ground and climb the trees and festoon the branches—a mass of purple and yellow bloom.

We **drove back to Calcutta along the river and crossed** the pontoon bridge. **A busy stream of humanity eddies** on the **entrances and flows over that bridge from morn**ing until night and far into the night. Up and down the banks of the river in either direction are row after row of stone steps, or ghats as they are called, which lead down to the water and on which swarms of people are bathing. They are scantily clad, or not clad at all, **and the** light reflects itself on their shining skin as it **does** on a polished bronze. The mysteries of life and **death are** there. **Not far** from the bridge cheek by jowl with **the bathing** ghats is the burning ghat where bodies are cremated and the ashes thrown into the Sacred river. The Hindu has a peculiar idea of sacredness and will call water sacred that is polluted by the filth of a sewer.

One Way Round the World

There is a wonderful beauty about fire, a splendor that flashes into existence and glows and flames and purifies and vanishes whence it came. A child instinctively reaches for the shining, waving glory that he thinks tangible and longs to feel, and it is only by worldly experience that he learns that fire is terrible and powerful. We forget that it is lovely. If to a blind man vision were suddenly given he would not gaze stolidly and indifferently at a curling flame. It would be a thing of transcendent, mysterious beauty.

So, it seems to me, the worn out bodies which the soul has left had best be wrapped in the destroying embrace of purifying fire. But oh, the pitifulness of the spectacle at the burning ghat in Calcutta. The rich leave life as they come into it—respectably, impressively—but the very poor die as they live—sordidly. There we saw poor creatures who had not accumulated enough money in their journey through the world to burn their wretched bodies when they left it. We drove up to the ghat and passing through a door and passageway stepped into an open quadrangle where the air was thick with smoke and there was a noise of crackling flames. The sight was horrifying.

In several places there were piles of charred wood, ashes and coals where funeral pyres had stood, and two others were still burning brightly. In one of them the body was almost consumed, but in the other it could be plainly seen. There hadn't been enough wood used to cover it. A half-dozen coolies were unconcernedly watching the burning of the body, which was too sick-

A Glimpse of the Ganges

ening for description, and occasionally poking the fire. We fled. Afterward at Benares I had quite a different impression of the Hindu ceremony, but I shall always think of that scene at Calcutta with a shudder.

One has only to turn off of the main streets to go slumming. The natives live in clusters of little mud huts, without windows or chimneys. The people love the streets and live in them. The women scour their lotas till they shine, with the dirt in the road, and the children tumble and play in it. For each cluster of houses there is a sunken pool or tank with steps leading down to it, filled with water as green as the banks. The drainage all runs into it and the people wash their clothes in it, bathe in it and drink from it. I think our boards of health at home would rest on their laurels if they could see the sanitary conditions under which these people live and thrive and multiply.

Our hotel in Calcutta was the Great Eastern, the best of a bad lot, and it was there we were first initiated into the mysteries of Indian hotel keeping. It was there, too, that we were introduced to chota hazri. Chota hazri isn't, as you may imagine, the name of some dignitary, but the name of the early breakfast. Perhaps I should have said that chota hazri was introduced to us. The ambition of the Indian hotel keeper seems to be to keep his guests eating all the time. Chota hazri in your bedroom at any hour before 10 o'clock, breakfast at 10, tiffin at 2, tea at 4, dinner at 8, and a dark doubt in your soul as to whether you'll find anything you can eat in any of them. After a try at all I've still felt like the small boy who said he had swallowed a hole. It is then that one's fancy lightly turns to thoughts of soda water, maple syrup, pop-corn, green corn, and all the edibles that float the stars and stripes.

As soon as we could lay hands on him, we secured the services of Narayam Lalla Every one in India travels with a servant. If you live here you are doomed to at least seven, for the man who washes the dishes shatters his caste if he blacks your shoes, and the man who pulls the punkah refuses to do errands, and so on. There are a few servants in the hotels, but their attention can not be depended upon. The only ones at the Great Eastern who displayed any energy were several that were perpetually swinging brushes over the slick marble corridors and making them more perilous than ever. Ah, I forgot another detachment. Whenever the head of our family stepped into his room and turned around, if he did so twenty times a day, he was confronted by a row of Hindus wearing the most injured expression, who had filed in after him. They all salaamed and extended their hands for a fee. We always knew what they wanted but what their services had been we were never able to learn. "The lean chested and leggy Hindu," the native has been called, and so he is, but perhaps not any more lean chested and leggy than the average Caucasian would look if he wore the Hindu's garb.

After you get your servant you have to take care not to step on him for he sleeps outside your door on the floor. At night the corridors are filled with sleeping

A Glimpse of the Ganges

figures. Narayam Lalla is a good looking, dark little fellow, who is intelligent and speaks English well. When he waits on us at the table, he wears a blue turban and a giddy red, yellow and green belt that satisfies our longing for local color. We have arrived at the dignity of Sahib and Memsahibs, master and mistress. Will the Sahib do this or would the Memsahibs like that, asks the Hindu. The Sahib and the Memsahibs went to Darjeeling and I will tell you about their journey.

There is probably no stranger or more beautiful railway journey in the world than that from Calcutta to Darjeeling. You may safely take a fan, an umbrella and a pair of skates. Leaving Calcutta in the afternoon, where the atmosphere is steaming and you are perspiring in muslins, you will be shivering under blankets twenty four hours later in the frosty air of Darjeeling. The first five hours of the ride was on an ordinary gauge road across the fertile plain of Bengal. We arrived at night on the banks of the Ganges and went immediately on board the little river steamer that was to carry us to the other bank. There was a lively crowd of Calcutta small boys who were going up to a boarding school in Darjeeling, and they kept us from growing over-sentimental as we might have done. A glorious moon sailed in the heavens and as we stood at the prow a fresh breeze blew from over the stream's bosom. The wide stretch of water looked lonely and sweetly peaceful. We followed the snaky current of the river winding from one far distant bank to the other, listening to the splash of the lead as it fell every few seconds into the water, while the sailors chanted the depth in the soft Hindustani tongue. The shoals are as treacherous there as they are farther down toward the sea and the pilot surveys and sounds along the channel every day in a small boat before he attempts to take the steamer through.

When we saw the Ganges again a great red sun was rising behind a rim of mist that lay along the horizon, and the yellow banks of sand and the placid water were tinted a faint pink. Between that clear moonlit night and that rosy dawn we had seen the most stupendous and the most gloriously beautiful mountains in the world. There is recompense for many of the ills of life on the day of days when one sees the sun rise on Kinchinjunga.

After we left the river boat we rode all night on a three-foot gauge, snatching as much sleep as we could in the rattling, swaying cars, which are provided with leather seats long enough to lie on. The traveler carries his own bedding, and a bundle of sheets and pillows and comforts is a part of one's impedimenta in India. There are always coolies to carry packages and valises, and one can travel conveniently with a great deal of baggage. In the morning we chota hazrid, and again pursued our journey. The gauge had shrunk another foot, and we found ourselves seated in armchairs in some queer little open cars behind a puffing, snorting little engine. It looked ridiculously small, but it pulled us sturdily up more than seven thousand feet. It is a remarkable railroad. The track winds and twists, mak-

ON THE WAY TO DARJEELING

A Glimpse of the Ganges

ing the figure 8 and the letter S many times and looping over itself several times. In one place, at what is called the reversing station, the train zigzags up a mountain slope and you can count the track five times. The chief marvel, though, is not the marvel of engineering, but the marvelous scenery that unrolls before the eyes. All day long the train winds in and out along the valleys, skirting dizzy precipices, on the edge of mighty gorges, opening up vista after vista of the grand wooded mountains that form the foot hills of the giant Himalayas.

Figures rarely are impressive, but the number of feet that these snow-crowned monarchs tower above the plain of Bengal far below gives an idea of their majesty. Janu, 25,300 feet; Kabur, 24,000 feet; Pandrin, 22,500 feet; Chomiano, 23,300 feet; Kinchinjunga, 27,500 feet, and Everest, 27,799 feet, a soaring peak that rises more than five miles above the sea.

After the train leaves Ghoom and rounds one of the flanking, lower mountains, Kinchinjunga is visible if the weather is clear. The clouds hung over it the day we went up, and our view of the long line of snows was postponed until an even more impressive occasion. As we went along we noticed curiously the strong Chinese cast of the features of the hill people. We were nearing the Chinese frontier, and in Darjeeling we saw many queer people of nationalities that I never happened to hear of—Lepchas, Nepalese, Bhutias, Thibetans—strange, outlandish creatures that are more like my idea of aborigines than any I have ever seen. The men and the women wear jewelry and pigtails, and are hard to tell apart by their dress. Stout little Nepalese women carried our trunks up the hill to the hotel on their backs. Some of the Bhutia women are handsome and Junoesque. The men are very often armed to the teeth with fierce knives, but they seem a kindly and friendly race of people. The women are loaded with barbaric gold and silver jewelry.

Everything around Darjeeling is on so grand a scale that the houses that fleck the hillsides look as if they had been spilled from some Noah's ark. It gave me always the impression of a toy town, though it is by no means small, and the houses when seen near by are many of them handsome summer houses. Mt. Everest is not visible from Darjeeling, and to see it an early morning excursion of six miles has to be made.

It seemed to me that I had scarcely closed my eyes when I heard a knock at my door and a husky voice called, "A quarter past three, Memsahib!" "All right," I said sleepily, while all my interest in Tiger Hills and Mt. Everests oozed out of my fingers' ends. But I rallied sufficiently to dress, putting on every warm garment I possessed, and went softly down the steps into the court of the hotel. The moon was shining brightly, and I could see a group of stalwart Bhutias standing near what I knew to be our sedan chairs and stamping to keep themselves warm. After a hasty breakfast by the light of a ghostly candle, we climbed into our chairs and at a signal the coolies picked us up and started up the valley with a long, rythmical, swinging step. They chattered and jested as gayly as

A Glimpse of the Ganges

the Japanese, and the moonlight twinkled on their earrings and polished finger rings. The moon hung full and resplendent. Long wisps of clouds lay low in the sky, and below I could distinguish the dark, undulating lines of the hills swathed in mist. Suddenly a mellow bell pealed out four strokes that echoed sweetly and quivered into silence. We went steadily onward and upward, along the edge of fearful precipices, past yawning gulches that sunk so far that the moonbeams were lost in their awesome depths. The great mountain slopes rose vast and mysterious all around us. The hours passed slowly, but did not lag. It was bitterly cold and we were chilled to the very marrow of our bones. We climbed out of the chairs and walked briskly, trying to stir our congealed blood. The blue moonlight was mingling with the yellowish glint of dawn. We hardly knew when the night ended and the day began. The stars grew dim and the gray blight which had seemed to lie on the grass and stunted shrubs whitened and sparkled. It was frost. Far up on the mountain side we passed row after row of melancholy chimneys crumbling into ruin and covered with lichens. They are the only souvenirs of the garrison which was once stationed at that bleak height. It was removed because so many of the men committed suicide. There is still a dak bungalow or rest station for travelers, but no one lives there. We had mounted 2,200 feet from Darjeeling. The sky above was clear, but a haze hung over the lower mountains. A last sharp incline was climbed by our panting coolies, and we were set down on the summit of Tiger Hill. A rim of the sun notched the horizon. Should we see the snows? Toward the west where they lay all was gray and lowering. All at once, high up above us, at what seemed half way to the zenith, the clouds were rent and I saw a bit of glittering, metallic white. "It is snow!" I cried. "It can't be!" exclaimed the others, "it is in the clouds." But as we spoke the rift grew wider, the gray cloud battalions wheeled and marched away, and as the sun was throwing his last beams on you at home we watched the sunrise on the snowy range of the Himalayas. Surely, the sun sees no fairer sight in all his journey.

Mt. Everest in the distance is plainly visible. It is a hundred and fifty miles away, and its glittering peak looks like a snowy tent. It is interesting as the highest point on the face of the earth, but the glory of that superb view belongs to peerless Kinchinjunga. The first bit that we had seen was indeed snow, and the mountain's icy summit towered high above it. Fleecy clouds lay along the base, making it hard to realize that there was an earthly foundation of granite for the heavenly, radiant vision that hung in the sky, as delicate as hoar frost on a window-pane, as iridescent as an opal's heart, as pure as its spotless snow fields. We watched it entranced for a time.

Alas! we were of the earth, earthy! Jack Frost tweaked our fingers and our noses and our toes, and we drank cognac and shivered and at last came regretfully away. The line of snows lay before us, clear and lovely for a time, but as we descended into the valley it was

A Glimpse of the Ganges

dimmed by the rising mist. Finally, the clouds piled up in foamy billows and it was gone. We came away the next day, and the gray wall of mist and clouds never lifted. I had had only one view of Kinchinjunga and the snowy range. I would not have had it otherwise if I could. I have with me the recollection of one perfect, glorious dawn, unblurred, ideal.

XIX

Benares, the Holy City of India

WHAT in the world shall I do for adjectives? I have recklessly used all of my superlatives on the charms of color in Japan and China and Ceylon, and here I am in India where there is such a wealth of hues that I should have to dip my pen in rainbow ink to do the subject justice. I wonder if the glow of tints would delight your eyes from morning till night as it does mine? Perhaps not, and you will weary of my rhapsodies.

India has seemed a dream realized, to me. Do you remember a collection of Verestchagin's pictures that was exhibited in many cities in the United States at the same time as the famous Angelus? They were as violent a contrast as one could imagine to the peaceful, hazy sunset, and the humble, devout peasants bowing at the sound of the vesper bell, which Millet's masterly touch made immortal—great glowing canvases whose story sometimes made you shudder, sometimes made you catch your breath in rapt admiration, and burned themselves into your memory. I supposed that the vivid figures, the deep azure skies, the white palaces with their latticed screens of lacy marble, were India

Benares, the Holy City of India

idealized; but they were India as it is. The old time splendor of the Mogul emperors is gone, a splendor perhaps never equaled in the world, and their deserted palaces are despoiled and crumbling. But enough of their magnificence has escaped the hands of invaders and destroyers to let the imagination cover them with the mantle of bygone glory. Such an enchantment hangs over them that even in the broad glare of noonday the mind's eye can see a bejeweled rajah, surrounded by his resplendent suite, walking on the noble verandas that overlook the river, and catch the glint of the bright eyes of the harem beauties peeping through a marble screen; or perhaps hear the sound of quaint music in the garden of the court, where the rosewater fountains splash and the wind sighs in the trees.

On the wall of the Hall of Audience, in the palace at Delhi—a perfect little gem of a structure, a marvel of milky marble and delicate tracery of color and gold—there is an inscription in the flowing, graceful Arabic characters. "If there be a paradise on earth, it is this, it is this, it is this." It was a happy choice for an inscription, but it gleams rather mockingly from the wall now when ugly British barracks crowd around it within the grand old fort, and clattering tourists click their heels on its marble floors and chatter idly under its graceful arches. It is a sad little commentary on the instability of mundane paradises. Even in the days when it was built it is probable that misery and unhappiness pressed as close around it as they do now.

But I would take you first to Benares, the holy city,

to which every Hindu's thoughts turn lovingly, where he longs to go and where he prays to die, that his ashes may be borne away on the loving bosom of the mother Ganges, and his soul be at peace.

Benares fringes the Ganges where the river bends itself into a beautiful blue bow; its stately palaces and temples, with their towers and domes and slender minarets, stretch along the crest of a hill that rises a hundred feet above the water. I can imagine how sweet that clear water has looked to the eyes of many a dusty, footsore, travel-stained pilgrim, who has traveled many a weary mile to the holy city. After threading painfully the narrow, tortuous, unfamiliar streets, he has stepped out at last on to one of the wide platforms that surround the palaces and has seen the sacred river, that will carry away his blackest sins, rippling at his feet.

Benares is one of the most ancient, if not the most ancient, of Indian cities, and is revered alike by those of the Hindu and the Buddhist faith. It was at Benares that Buddha preached his first sermon and sent his missionaries forth to Ceylon, China, Burmah, Nepal and Thibet. There is a tradition, too, that one of the Wise Men of the East who brought presents to the infant Jesus at Jerusalem, was a Rajah of Benares. Buddhism has been superseded by Brahmanism in India, but there is a third great religion of the East represented in the holy city, whose temple is the crowning one of them all, whose slender minarets seem to pierce the sky—the Mohammedan mosque built by the hated Aurangzeb on the very foundation of a Hindu temple which he destroyed.

BRAHMIN WORSHIPING

Benares, the Holy City of India

It appears that monkeys and parrots get along amicably in comparison with Hindus and Mohammedans. They hate one another with a deep and undying hatred and to this day indulge in fierce and bloody battles, even within the walls of their sanctuaries. In some places laws have been passed which forbid Mohammedans to enter Hindu temples and Hindus to enter Mohammedan mosques.

I describe Benares to myself as satisfying, but it may be that this word would have no meaning for others. There was nothing there that I would have had changed, nothing jarring, nothing discordant.

We rode all night and well into the day going from Calcutta to Benares, through a parched, dry country where the thirsty earth seemed to cry for water. It was the beginning of the famine district. There were a few pitiful stunted fields of grain with an occasional green patch starred with white poppy blossoms. There has been no rain in India for two years, and with the failure of the crops has come distress and famine. The mass of the people are so poor and the population so dense that they can have little or nothing laid by—not for the proverbial rainy day, but the dry day. "If the next monsoon does not bring rain, heaven help us," said the gentleman from Madras.

Laborers earn only three, four and five annas a day— six, eight and ten cents of our money—women and children two and one anna. In some parts of India families live on an average of less than one anna—two cents— a day, for each member. This year the number of people who are suffering actual want runs into millions. I have hardened my heart to many things, but no one who has any of the leaven of compassion in his soul could see a man or a woman or a little child who is starving, without distress. The dreadful shadows of human beings whom I have seen tottering along the streets haunt me in my dreams. I did not know that the spark of life would linger in such emaciated, starved bodies. We give to as many as we can, but we can reach so few! The Hindus themselves are shockingly callous to the distress of the poor, and the sleek, well-fed merchants and jewelers pass the poor, suffering wretches without so much as a glance of compassion. In many places we saw hordes of people employed on what is called relief work, work that is instituted by the government to give employment to the suffering. They are the most miserable, lean, hollow-eyed people that I've ever seen. Mothers are carrying heavy basket-loads of earth on their heads, while they hold a baby on their hips. Fathers, too, carry children, and little things hardly past babyhood trudge along with their load of earth on their heads. They are earning the anna a day that keeps them from starvation.

Benares looked beautiful as we came into it. We saw beyond a stretch of yellow scintillating sand, the blue bend of the river and the long line of noble palaces. They were far away, but they stood out with the distinctness that is peculiar to the Indian atmosphere. On the ghats and on the river bank we could distinguish a lazy stir of human life. At the station there were

ON THE BANKS OF THE GANGES AT BENARES

Benares, the Holy City of India

crowds of pilgrims in blues, yellows, greens and purples, with bells on their fingers and rings on their toes! Their bundles of luggage were as gay as themselves.

We drove often in the dry, dusty, glaring streets. Our landaus in India were worthy of a nabob. We had coachmen and footmen and syce or runners to clear the way. To be sure, the elegance was sometimes a bit dingy and faded, but that doesn't matter in the East. Inside the ramshackle gharries you often catch a glimpse of some Oriental family resplendent in tinsel, satin and embroidery. All the rajahs and wealthy men of India pride themselves on having a home in the holy city; there are many fine palaces and dwellings belonging to this or that maharajah or personage of note.

It appears that maharajahs have their troubles. I heard a story of two of them which amused me, but I carelessly allowed their names to slip my mind. We will call them Maharajah Number 1 and Maharajah Number 2. Maharajah Number 1 is the ruler of the province in which Benares lies. At the time of the visit of the Prince of Wales to India some years ago Maharajah Number 1 arranged for his little son to sit on the left of the Prince. Maharajah Number 2 pushed the little fellow away and took the seat himself. Maharajah Number 1 was furious, and from that day to this, when Maharajah Number 2 comes to Benares, he has to camp outside the city and hustle through his prayers at the shrines in undignified haste, leaving within twenty-four hours.

There are many shrines scattered through the open

and more modern part of the city. They have elaborately carved spires that are flecked with gold spots. Covered with icing, they would make beautiful wedding cakes. The rows of houses in which the humbler people live have walls of mud covered with whitewash as dingy as the bedraggled white garments of the coolies. They are decorated with crude frescoes.

One day as we were driving our attention was arrested by the sound of a terrific tom-toming that seemed to be coming toward us. The horses started uneasily and we stopped to await developments. From around the corner between the hot, glaring walls wound a brilliant procession. First came the drummers pounding their tom-toms. Next a tall, dark man of twenty-five or thirty. He was dressed in a gorgeous suit of green and blue and surrounded by a flock of yellow-robed attendants. "He's a bridegroom," said Lalla, and we leaned forward to look with an added interest. Back of him came the little bride guarded by another blaze of yellow followers. She was a little thing, certainly not more than seven or eight years old. The upper part of her body was muffled up in a thick yellow veil, but below her full tinseled skirts peeped out and we could see her little brown feet heavy with massive anklets. "Ah," sighed the Wise One, "what a child she is." Just a moment and the procession was gone, hidden by another bend in the street. The tom-toms sounded faintly and more faintly and died away. Lalla was married when he was eleven, he says, and his wife was seven.

A LITTLE TAMIL BRIDE

Benares, the Holy City of India

I should only weary you by telling you of the round of temples that we visited. They were all interesting and curious and all full of pilgrims from every corner of India. The Monkey Temple is a red sandstone building, ornately carved. Monkeys were climbing all around and we bought some popcorn for them and some half-starved dogs that were skulking about. We were received by a Hindu priest, with a red smear of paste on his forehead, who wore a dilapidated blue velvet suit.

"Salaam! Salaam! Salaam!" cried a chorus of loathsome beggars, thrusting their disgusting deformities into our very faces. We speedily had enough of the Monkey Temple and hastened away without stopping to ask the customary desultory questions about the history, which we always promptly forget.

The Golden Temple, where the terrible god Siva is worshiped, is the holy of holies of Benares. Siva is worshiped under a variety of forms, always gruesome and awful. He is a creator and destroyer, the ruler of evil spirits, ghosts and vampires. Siva is the god of the ascetics, a strange, weird sect of men who wear no clothes and smear their bodies with ashes. Their matted hair hangs in strings. Some of them live on food too nauseous to mention. These disgusting creatures swarm in Benares and give you an unpleasant start if you come upon them unexpectedly around a dark corner. There are so many different types of religious men that the subject is an endless puzzle.

XX

A Wise Man of India

WE went one day to see a famous old wise man. He is supported by some rajah or other and lives in a leafy garden, the greenest spot in Benares. We entered the garden by a door set in the wall and walked to the center of it, where there was a pavilion. Beyond, at the other side of the garden, we could see a dwelling and out of it there came a weird little old man, bent, hairy and toothless. He had wound a bit of drapery around him in deference to our prejudices, but otherwise he was garmentless. His cheeks and lips were sunken and his face a mesh of wrinkles; his eyes glowed like two coals of fire, the most wonderful eyes I've ever seen, dark, piercing, and apparently filled with a boundless benevolence. They had the flash and brilliancy of youth; they lighted his kindly old face and made it beam with good-will. He greeted us cordially. Lalla acted as interpreter.

"Ask him a question," he suggested. As a rule, I have plenty of momentous questions by me, but, of course, at that crisis they all deserted me. "Ask him," I said, "ask him whether the next year is going to be a happy one for me." The little old man looked at me

HOLY MAN OF BENARES

A Wise Man of India

and his twinkling eyes smiled. He lifted his hand as if in blessing. "The dear young lady's fortune is all good," he said. Then he suddenly seized my hand in his and drew me with him. I followed wonderingly. We went along a shady walk, where the birds were singing and stopped before a rose bush. It was filled with beautiful blossoms, pink on the edges of their full petals, with a tint of wine in their hearts. My guide chattered to himself softly in his own tongue as he gathered a bunch of them, then he handed them to me, again with that rare smile. We went on to a little building of marble, and mounting the steps and peeping in as he directed, I saw a marble statue of himself. It was utterly unlike him. A likeness of such eyes would have to be molded from sunbeams, but I affected pleasure to please him. He laughed softly and again taking my hand we went down the steps and back to our party. An attendant brought us a book in which we put our autographs. There were a number of American names there, and Mark Twain remarked with a scrawl that a good many of his countrymen seem to be traveling this year. I thought that one needed the reputation of a Mark Twain to make that remark worth writing. The old man then presented us with a book containing his picture and some of his writing, and we came away leaving him standing in the sunlight and extending his hands in friendly farewell. I don't know whether he tells all young ladies that their fortune is good and gathers roses for them as he did for me. If he does they probably remember him as pleasantly as I do. All day long the fragrance of the roses carried me back to the green garden and the wonderful, kindly face of the old philosopher.

At the Golden Temple, so called because its spires are sheathed with plates of gold, we were allowed a glimpse of a crowd of devout worshipers but were not allowed to profane the temple with our footsteps. It was a smelly, dirty place into which I had no desire to venture. Quite near it there is a Mohammedan mosque, built as an insult to the Hindu faith, but its worshipers have lost possession of the court yard and have to enter the mosque by a side door. In this court, there is a brilliant collection of people. Many weary pilgrims are sleeping stretched out in the sun on the ground and covered with a blanket of cotton cloth. The children are scampering and shouting as they play. The small merchants have spread their wares on the ground and are on the alert for customers. The beggars chant their eternal "Backsheesh, Memsahib," "Backsheesh, Memsahib." The women stand about in idly graceful poses or gossip together in a patch of shade. This indolent heterogeneous crowd swirls around all the temples in the holy city and is not the least of its charms. Between the Golden Temple and the Mosque is the Well of Knowledge. It is under a canopy of red sandstone, and the holy water is ladled out by the priests in return for offerings. The water is fairly thick, filthy and putrid from the rotting flowers that have been thrown into it, but the people drink it eagerly. The floor is dirty, and I don't think anything about the place has

AN ASCETIC

A Wise Man of India

ever been cleaned. As you walk around you are continually invited to step out of the way while a sacred cow goes by. The passage ways (one can hardly call them streets) are so narrow, that there is barely space for a fat cow to squeeze by as you flatten yourself against the wall. The streets that surround the temples are full of little shops where idols and gew-gaws are indiscriminately mixed up. In one place there is a Cow Temple where cows are presented as an offering. They stand in stalls around an open quadrangle, some of them old and decrepit, some well groomed and young. The floor is filthy and the connection between such a place and sanctity impossible to grasp. It was when in full retreat from this uninviting quarter that I almost ran into one of those ghostly ash-bedaubed ascetics.

These are not the places I had in mind when I called Benares satisfying. They are curious and deeply interesting, a perfect revelation of the tremendous difference in the habits and beliefs and customs of nations, but they do not appeal to one's æsthetic sense. The continual appeal is to one's olfactory nerves. The old man who followed his nose wouldn't need a guide in Benares.

It is the river that is ever fascinating, ever lovely, ever grand. I've told you of the beautiful blue bow and the line of stately palaces and temples. When you are floating down the stream on one of the comfortable river boats they tower so high above you that they seem to notch the sky. Below them descend great flights of stone steps or ghats that are broken in places into platforms and shrines. Down to the water's edge they come in imposing files. In some places the foundations have given away and the steps and the buildings lean at many angles, but they are of such noble proportions that they are always grand. Half closing my eyes, I liked to imagine a procession of the palmy days, a resplendent rajah dressed in the rich brocades of Benares and Ahmedabad, with woof of silk and warp of gold, glittering jewels from Ceylon, perfumes of Araby, superb canopies from Kashmir, all the magnificence of the East. Yet there is no need to go back to the old days for beauty. From one end of the river front to the other the ghats are alive with people. They are crowded together and make a belt bordering the river that glows and burns with color as vivid as the gay Dutch tulip beds that carpet the earth around Haarlem. The rising sun twinkles in thousands of shining brass lotas from which the people are drinking and in which they carry away the holy water. They bathe and pray alternately. Big shield-shaped umbrellas of straw throw spots of shade. Long strips of colored cloth float like banners in the breeze and are afterwards deftly wound into garments and turbans by their owners. Picturesque figures carrying large earthen water jars pass up and down the steps. The people come from every corner of India and there is every variety of costume. The women from Jeypore with gorgeous shawls, full tinseled skirts and massive jewelry are the most curious. Probably there is no more wonderful sight in the world. Up and down the ghats all day long streams this endless

A Wise Man of India

procession, where for centuries the sun has risen and set on worshiping Brahmans. At the burning ghat we came upon a strange sight. High upon the hill was a temple with the usual line of descending steps lined with rows of dark figures in bright colored draperies listlessly watching the ceremony. The peculiar stones that break the lines of the steps are suttee stones, where widows were formerly burned alive. Down below, lying half in and half out of the water, was a still white figure stretched on a cot of rushes. On the breast there was a bunch of flowers and a red substance which had stained the winding sheet when the body was dipped in the sacred river. Just above the water's edge was a pile of ashes with a few white charred bones lying in it and a little farther a pile of logs was blazing merrily, though the white feet of the body were still untouched by the flames. Men are wrapped in a white winding sheet and the women in red. They are burned very soon after they die, while the bodies are still limp. A near relative accompanies the body and drives a bargain with the priest for the fire which is to light the funeral pyre. He pays according to his means, and sometimes when a maharajah or rich man dies the priest is paid a thousand rupees for the fire. The rich are burned with sandal wood and the flames are extinguished at the last with milk. The charge for the ordinary wood for the poor is small and the friendless are burned at the government's expense. They are brought to the ghat in a winding sheet of common sacking, lashed to a pole. Early in the morning you can see the coolies washing out the ashes in baskets looking for the gold and silver ornaments which the dead have worn. When the body is placed on the pyre the relative takes the bundle of blazing sticks which the priest has given him and walks five times around it lighting the wood under the head and the feet. Then he retires to the steps until the pyre is consumed. I told you of the revolting sight at the ghat in Calcutta, but in Benares the ceremony is impressive and beautiful.

Benares is famous for brass and brocades. The brocades are rich gold and silk fabrics worth their weight in gold. We went to the street of the brass workers, where there is an endless variety of chased brass articles, a very few of them fine, most of them clumsy and ugly. The narrow street rings with the blow of the hammers and the clinks of the chisels. The prices for the work are surprisingly low, and you can get a vase as big as an umbrella stand for a few rupees, if it be to your taste. I contented myself with some miniature lotas and a delicately chiseled cup.

. . . .

At Lucknow, which is interesting to every Englishman as the scene of the dreadful massacre of 1857, we drove in the bazars and visited the sights as usual. The old Residency, where the imprisoned garrison was kept so many weary, anxious months, is now a picturesque ruin, and it and the buildings surrounding it are set in a green and flowery garden that is a relief to the eyes after the glaring heat and choking dust of the streets. The days are hot and dusty, but the evenings and nights

PAVILION AT LUCKNOW

are cool and starlit. India's "winter" is drawing to a close. Very soon the heat can be rendered endurable only by the **punkah,** a long swinging **fan** suspended **over** one's head and manipulated by a native. "The day punkahs begin in March," said Mrs. Fleming, "and the night punkahs the last of April. One must have an old person, the older the better, for a punkah wallah, for the boys and girls go to sleep." Mrs. Fleming is a young and charming Englishwoman, the wife of Captain Fleming, and only sister of Rudyard Kipling. I told her with what added enjoyment I had read her brother's stories since I had been in India, and asked her if she wrote herself. She was a singularly sweet and sunny person, and she laughed lightly as she replied: "Oh, I scribble a little, and I'm soon to have a story published called the 'Pinchbeck Goddess.'"

The Museum at Lucknow is interesting. It has many beautiful fabrics woven and embroidered with thread of gold, and I saw there a gold and jeweled robe and turban which gave me an idea of the glittering magnificence of a maharajah in robes of state. In another place we saw a gallery of portraits of moguls loaded with jewels as big as birds' eggs.

XXI

Agra and its Taj Mahal

IN Lucknow we stopped at Hill's Imperial Hotel, imperial in name only, but the best that is to be found. All the hotels in India are down-at-the-heel establishments, where the food is fair and the rooms arranged in what seems the most senseless fashion—three or four barny rooms to each suite with dirty floor coverings and grimy crockery, when one well-appointed room would be much more convenient and desirable. In one small room where there is only a wardrobe for furnishing, you are likely to find a carpet, while you walk to your bath in the bath-room over rough and, I need not say, icy flagstones. Arriving in the middle of the night, after telegraphing for rooms, you will find the bed unmade and no water in the water-jug. The attendants are few and your own servant does most of the work. But like a certain well-known old gentleman, the hotels are, after all, not so black as they are painted. All unite in reviling them, and you are prepared for something worse than you really get.

We haggled a little with the dealers who haunt the veranda at Hill's. Bargaining is the poetry of trade to the Oriental. The fakirs and jugglers and vendors of

Agra and its Taj Mahal

things we didn't want were persistent and insistent and we afterward found that the prices they asked were outrageous. The Indian silver is engaging. The boxes and bowls that they offer for sale are roughly chased but they have a pretty style. I was beguiled by some little boxes chased with the jungle pattern and a powder box with little doubled up Buddhas neatly arranged in decorative medallions. The dealer has a scale and weighs the article against so many rupees, then you pay from four to six annas, eight to twelve cents extra, according to the work, for each rupee in weight.

For fear you'll imagine a rupee a glittering gold coin as big as a butter plate, I'll tell you that they are silver coins and that it would take three of them to equal in value our tiny gold dollar. I shall never be impressed as I used to be at the mention of fabulous fortunes of rupees. The "jungle pattern," which is a favorite, is an ingenious design of palm trees and the various animals of the jungle, particularly elephants. These huge and gentle beasts walking sedately along the roads, carrying large burdens, are a delightfully Oriental touch of the landscapes. There is an Indian proverb that says: "If you could load him standing, an elephant would carry the world." They have to be loaded when they are lying down, of course, and can not rise with too heavy a load. One day when we were driving past the Great Imambara we saw a huge elephant coming toward us and stopped to take his photograph. The keeper saw us, and halting the old fellow he clambered down over his head, holding on by his ear while the elephant sagaciously lifted his knee to make a last step to the ground. They are such stupid-looking creatures, but they are docile and extremely intelligent. It costs five rupees a day at present prices to feed them—a large sum for this country—and they can only be kept by rich men. They eat sugar-cane, bran and hay and are very fond of a sweetened dough called chowpatty, at least that is the way it sounds. The elephant is allowed a certain number of cakes a day, and when he receives them he counts them over carefully. If he hasn't received all he is entitled to he trumpets loudly and will not be appeased until the full number is made up. Occasionally keepers have been killed for deceiving them. The elephants will pick up the smallest silver coin with their trunks and hand it to their masters.

Our journey through the bazars was not an unannoyed pleasure, fascinating as they are. The shops of the bazars are box-like little establishments where the dusky merchants sit cross-legged on the floor. They smoke their pipes and take the busy days calmly. In the street there is the usual crowd of lounging natives, and we passed many rows of travel-stained pilgrims on their way to Benares. They carried their belongings in two baskets decorated with tufts of peacock feathers swung over their shoulders, and each one had a brass lota in which to bring away the holy water. My eyes followed, too, the beautiful, soft-hued embroidered shawls that were draped around the picturesque Kashmiris, and the gorgeous turbans of the tall, fierce looking Afghans. The turbans are long strips of rich material

BULLOCK CART, LUCKNOW

Agra and its Taj Mahal

wound around a peaked center of gold embroidery. Mr. Jacob tells me that when he takes his stunning Afghan servant to Paris and to London the pretty girls take the servant for an Indian prince and Mr. Jacob for the valet. He is in truth a princely fellow; tall, dark-skinned, fine-looking, with an elegant turban and a resplendent suit of dark blue and gold cut in the chest protector fashion that obtains in India, that is, the coat is cut with a kind of yoke that is the shape of the chest protectors that adorn the show windows of the country drug stores. The winding of a turban is a fine art. None of them are sewed or even pinned, and they are dexterously wound in different forms to indicate the caste of the owner. They are sometimes red, sometimes blue, orange, variegated, and often white, usually very large. The coolies make their turbans of coarse white cotton cloth, but a rich merchant will have a snowy headgear that is light as down, made of a wonderful cobwebby muslin that is woven in Dacca, near Darjeeling, and is sometimes worth its weight in gold.

At the shop of Ganaisha Lal, in Agra, a famous dealer in rare and lovely goods, I saw many exquisite fabrics that are not to be found often. When I first went there I was waited on by a suave clerk who called me "Your Ladyship," and immediately produced his book of recommendations from maharajahs and Vanderbilts. One of the trials of life is that ubiquitous book of testimonials from Lord and Lady This and Millionaire That, which is constantly thrust under your unwilling gaze. Afterward, I was waited upon by

One Way Round the World

Ganaisha Lal himself, a handsome Indian, who is said to have, among a collection, an American wife. He showed me many bolts of the filmy Dacca muslins which are most poetically named,—running water, dew of evening, woven air, etc. They are said to be invisible in water but I did not see them immersed. They can only be bought by the bolt, which is worth a small fortune, and I could not get the small piece that I coveted for a specimen of the wondrous skill in the art of weaving. Three pieces were given to the Prince of Wales when he visited India. They were twenty yards long and one yard wide and weighed three and a half ounces. Tavernier, the French traveler, who visited India a couple of centuries ago, and who wrote many quaint and interesting letters that tell of the wonders of those days and the splendor of the Mogul courts, speaks of a muslin turban thirty yards long, woven at Dacca, which was packed in a jeweled cocoanut.

In China we bought a bolt of gauzy grass linen that has been a continual delight to me, but I wasn't at all tempted by the Dacca muslins. In my practical eye they had a quality described by that deadly word "stringy," and I decided that they could be put to no good use. How that last word would offend my artistic friend Mr. Colonna, who has in his possession so many rare and lovely things and who winces at the suggestions of well-meaning people of ways to make use of his treasures. (To use them would be a desecration.) He has a box of fine fabrics from all corners of the earth that are carefully folded and put away. Occasionally he takes

Agra and its Taj Mahal

them out and looks them over, handling them lovingly, almost reverentially, before they are again laid away in the box. He assured me that they are a panacea for all his ills.

Ganaisha Lal had many fine Kashmir shawls, ring shawls they are called, because it is said that they can be drawn through a finger ring. The finest ones are white and perfectly plain, but the texture is exquisite. They are woven of camel's hair, in hand looms, and their soft surface is a caress to the touch. These shawls are narrow and several yards long, and they come folded and sewed on the edges. Before paying forty or fifty dollars for a fine one, it is safer to have it opened and examine it carefully. The wily Kashmiri has been known to weave a fine strip on the ends and fill in the middle with an ordinary quality.

But I have wandered far from the Bazar street in Lucknow, and I'll only take you back there for a moment. The street is so narrow that our carriage blocked the way, and we were soon surrounded by a mob of howling merchants who wanted to sell us their wares. Words are lost on these fellows, and a stout stick brandished threateningly is the only thing that will keep them away. I extracted an embroidered handkerchief from the crush and wanted several dozen more, but we got out of the din, intending to go back on foot and incognito, if possible. We never did, however, and the thing I remember best about the bazars at Lucknow was the brave array of spangled, tinseled shoes in the quarter of the shoe dealers.

One Way Round the World

Our stay at Cawnpore was mercifully short. We went on to Agra in the evening, and I arrived at the station with my spirits at zero. It was in Cawnpore that we saw so many desperate, starving people, men, women, children and animals, that were walking skeletons, half fainting from hunger. That look of dumb suffering in their ghostly eyes haunted me in my dreams. What grim torture it must be to a man who is dying for want of food to see it around him in the shops and to beg fruitlessly of the sleek and well-fed for money to buy it. The people in the cities are not in as pitiable a plight, however, at present as those in the outlying country districts. If the Hindus would eat flesh the famine would not be so severe, but they will die first. They will not take life either, and they allow their wretched live stock to starve with themselves. On account of the famine it is an unfortunate year to visit India. We would always find poverty, but not such distress.

There seemed to be an accumulation of depressing sights that day, for the round of places which the tourist is doomed to visit are the scenes of the ghastly massacres of 1857. Of a garrison of more than nine hundred souls only four escaped. We saw the ghat where the boats started on the river and were fired at by the treacherous natives who had granted a truce. The four men who escaped lay in the water for hours. The natives carried out the orders of that inhuman wretch, Nana Sahib, the leader of the mutiny, and brutally murdered men, women and children. The well into which the

DOMES OF THE PEARL MOSQUE, AGRA

Agra and its Taj Mahal

defenseless women and children were thrown, the dead with the dying, till the water was red with blood, is now in the center of a park. The well itself is surrounded by a large octagonal screen, beautifully carved in stone, and just over the well is a lovely marble statue by Marochetti, an angel with folded wings standing at the foot of a cross. Over the gate is the inscription, "These are they which came out of great tribulation." In a little cemetery near by are the graves of several hundred people who perished. The gravestones tell the story of their death. They died so young!

In the Memorial Chapel we were shown around by a British soldier of the Seventy-fourth regiment, in a gay red coat and plaid trousers. He spoke always of the "massacree" and how people were massacreed. Altogether, his accent and grammar were terrific, and he made his speech headlong without a comma or a period in the whole of it. He acted as a lever on my sinking spirits. I was also irrepressibly and unbecomingly tickled by a tablet in the floor which announced that 300 feet of the flooring was laid in memory of a certain man. How deliciously unconventional to receive your memorial by the square yard.

.   .   .   .   .   .

"You must not see the Taj first," said Lalla, "or you will care for nothing else." So we arranged the climax properly, and went first to see the other sights of Agra. The whole of it is delightful, and Agra contains many of the most beautiful buildings that we have seen. Whether you are gazing on the massive red sandstone walls of the old fort, or the milky marble arches of the dazzling Pearl Mosque, the delicate, frost-like carvings of the tomb of Itmad-ud-Daulah or the glorious Taj Mahal itself, your eyes are everywhere delighted.

Itmad-ud-Daulah was the father-in-law and prime minister of the Emperor Jehangir. Jehangir had his faults, I believe, but he did his best and he built a mausoleum for his father-in-law which is a masterpiece of delicacy and beauty. Jehangir's wife was not born to the purple, but she was wondrously beautiful and found favor in the emperor's eyes. It was Jehangir who caused a chain to be hung from the citadel to the ground. This chain communicated with a cluster of golden bells in his own chamber, and any suitor might apprise the emperor of his demands for justice without the intervention of the courtiers.

The tomb of Itmad-ud-Daulah lies across the broad river Jumna on which Agra is situated, and is reached by a long and rickety pontoon bridge. The bridge is crowded with bullock carts and people bringing in the country produce, and on the yellow sand of the river bed all Agra's washing seems to be spread. The tombs and temples of India are always surrounded by an imposing wall with four great gates, usually of rich-colored red sandstone. These gates are beautiful in themselves, but they are apt—one can hardly say to be overlooked—but to pass unnoticed because of the greater beauty of the building that they enclose. Entering through one of these lofty and beautiful portals you reach the tomb, a marvel of pure, delicately carved

PIERCED MARBLE SCREENS AT AGRA

Agra and its Taj Mahal

marble and pietra dura work. It has all the charm of a miniature, and in comparison with more splendid monuments remains a masterpiece of daintiness. It seemed to me more appropriate for a woman's memory than the stately Taj Mahal. The lower part has beautiful panels of pietra dura and wonderful carved marble screens, and up above there is a lovely canopy screened by this same delicately carved marble, through which the sunlight creeps, mellow and golden. You will find that I speak often of these pierced screens, for they are found everywhere and are so rarely beautiful. In the shops you can buy miniatures of them in marble, exquisitely carved. Pietra dura is a Florentine art introduced into India a century or two ago by the Italian workmen whom the Mogul emperors brought to India. And so it happens that you may buy in far-away India the very same marble monstrosities, if I may be so bold as to speak my mind, that fill the little shops along the Arno in Florence. The pietra dura work is very effective for buildings, very beautiful, indeed, but in the small articles known as souvenirs it is hideous.

In the fort at Agra, that noble pile of sandstone whose massive outer walls are still another triumph of Shah Jehan, you may dream many idle hours away. There is still enough left of the splendid apartments, beautiful courts, marble verandas and balconies to make the dream of the unparalleled magnificence of the Moguls almost a reality. The Moti Masjid or Pearl Mosque is one of the gems that the fort encloses. It is a mosque of pure white marble and its three domes of beautiful proportions probably suggested the Pearl that was chosen for its name. It is an ideal house of prayer, but when we saw it the inlaid figures on the marble floor, pointing toward Mecca and intended to be filled by pious Mohammedans, were empty, and there were no worshipers. In one place in the palace is a marble balcony overhanging a court once filled with water where the emperor amused himself at fishing. In another are the latticed screens through which the ladies of the harem looked down on a bazar and bought of the merchants what pleased their fancy. In still another are the squares of black and white marble set in the floor where they played chess and parcheesi with living figures. Here are the rose water fountains and the sumptuous bath-rooms, set with a thousand tiny mirrors, where the ladies bathed. There is the great square where the elephant fights were held. On the right is the Jasmine Tower, which is said to have been the boudoir of the chief sultana, on the left the noble open portico where stands the black marble throne. It is cracked, and stained with what the guide calls blood. They say that the marble cracked and blood gushed forth when the throne was stepped on by a Mahrattan invader. Everything suggests a bit of fascinating history over which the glamour of romance hangs. You see the place where Shah Jehan was confined for many years by his heartless son Aurangzeb who dethroned and imprisoned him, and on one of the balconies the spot is pointed out where he is said to have been carried when

ARCHES IN THE PEARL MOSQUE

Agra and its Taj Mahal

dying that his eyes might rest last on the peerless Taj Mahal.

The view from this portico is grand, never-to-be-forgotten. The stately castle walls stretch away to the right and left and the delicate marble towers and balconies of the palace that rise above them contrast strangely with the massive frowning battlements. Far below there are some trees with groups of camels and people lying in the shade. Beyond is the blue curve of the Jumna with its border of yellow sand, and across it, delicately misty, are the minarets and dome of the Taj. This rounded dome has often been compared to a pearl, but I like better to think of it as an airy soap bubble that has been moored to earth and frozen into stone. There is the ethereal charm about it that the iridescent, shining bubble has.

This most famous of mausoleums was built by the Emperor Shah Jehan for his beloved wife, the beautiful Mumtez-i Mahal. Never were there more devoted royal lovers and never has a love had such a rare perpetuation. It is a sweet story. There, in the beautiful garden which the queen loved in life, she lies in death beside her lord and lover. He built for her the most splendid mausoleum that the world has known and he dedicated it "To the Memory of an Undying Love." And truly everything that is lovely in love seems to have found form and shape in that wondrous structure. There is a singular purity and sweetness about it that impresses the most careless. It is solid marble, but it is delicate; it is grand, but it is graceful; it is elaborate in detail, but it has an effect of beautiful simplicity. It is an illustration of the saying that the Moguls designed like giants and finished like jewelers.

  I have a regretful feeling that I can not carry you with me in my enthusiasm for this matchless "poem in stone," this "blossoming in marble." I could tell you the millions of rupees that it cost, the number of feet that its snowy minarets tower in the air, the width of the stately sandstone platforms on which it stands, but neither figures nor words would make you feel its beauty or catch your breath as you would do if it suddenly lay before your eyes. It is the magnet of Agra that draws one to it again and again in every idle hour, in the fresh morning, at azure noon, at rosy sunset, by silver moonlight, to find it ever fair, ever serene, ever lovely. If I could have a wish for you all it should be that you might walk in the green garden, where the bulbul, the sweet voiced nightingale of the East, sings to the rose, where the jasmine and the orange blossoms spread sweet fragrance and where the lovely marble tomb radiates tenderness and beauty and purity. You would forget yourself there for a season and you would be the better for it.

THE TAJ MAHAL

XXII

A Modern Prince of India

AH, I might write for a week without describing half of the glories of Agra, and so I might write for a week without describing half of my delightful acquaintance with Mr. Jacob. There is perhaps no better known figure throughout India, and I feel that I am again in the domain of the unreal when I begin to write about this remarkable man. Mr. F. Marion Crawford has made his fame world wide, for it is Mr. Jacob who is the original of the Mr. Isaacs in Crawford's fascinating story of that name. In private life he is Mr. A. M. Jacob, of Simla, India, a millionaire dealer in jewels, and a polished and brilliant gentleman. He is a Turk by birth and came to India when a boy. I listened with deep interest to his story of the day when he asked his mother for a silver coin to buy some lettuce and then ran away and began his venturesome journey to the East. He did not see his mother for years, until he was a grown man, and no longer young, but when he went to meet her he was careful to go armed with a big basket of lettuce. They had feared the strain for her, but when he said, "Here mother, here is your basket of lettuce," she burst out laughing and the danger was past. I shall never be able to choose what is most interesting in Mr. Jacob's conversation. He talks entertainingly of anything and everything and I'm sure that the veriest platitudes would become absorbing from his lips. There is a remarkable magnetism about the man, and when he speaks his wonderful dark eyes flash and glow with intelligence and feeling. Perhaps he talks most entertainingly of jewels, the great jewels of the world whose history is the history of kings and queens, and the rise and fall of empires.

One morning we drove with Mr. Jacob to the Secundra, the magnificent tomb of Akbar the Great, which is a few miles distant from Agra. It is another great pile of red sandstone and milky marble guarded by the same massive wall and towering gates and surrounded by the same flowery, fragrant garden. The clear Indian sky was never more beautifully blue. The air was balmy and bright colored birds were flying in the air and twittering in the trees. The monkeys were chattering too, and scolding violently. A cunning little brown boy offered us a bouquet of orange blossoms and went away with a silver bit squeezed in his little brown fist. The grave of Akbar is simply marked as are other Indian graves by a raised slab of marble. The grave itself is in a vault below the level of the ground, but in each story of the mausoleum, just above the grave, there is a corresponding slab of marble to mark the spot under which the grave lies. At the very top, within a quadrangle enclosed by carved marble screens and near the gravestone, is a low marble pillar on which the

A Modern Prince of India

famous Kohinoor reposed for many years. I perched myself on the pillar while Mr. Jacob told me the stirring history of the gem and I should not dare hint at the extravagant compliment which I there received. It is a story of love and intrigue, how rajahs played at chess for a beauty of the harem, or zenana as they say in India, how she twice saved the game for her master, how he finally lost it and gave her as a forfeit to his opponent. Then she revenged herself by revealing that the hiding place of the wonderful diamond was in her master's turban. The second rajah secured possession of the turban by a ruse, and when he unwound it the great diamond fell into his hand. "Ah," he cried breathlessly. "It is a Koh-i-Noor" (mountain of light), and it was thus that the diamond was named. "It is an unlucky gem, though," said Mr. Jacob. "It never brought the Indian princes anything but misfortune, and each time that the Queen of England has worn it she has met with some mishap." Mr. Jacob is the man who lately sold the Imperial Diamond to the Nizam of Hyderabad for $1,500,000. Isn't that a figure to make one's eyes bulge! I saw a model of it, a flawless stone that weighs a hundred and eighty carats. It was once in the possession of Dom Pedro, of Brazil, from whom it was bought by a syndicate. It was sold by the syndicate to Mr. Jacob and he in turn sold it to the Nizam. The affair got into the courts and after having been long and bitterly contested was finally decided in Mr. Jacob's favor. I will tell you the story of the difficulty as he told it to me. He sold the diamond to the

One Way Round the World

Nizam for £300,000 as a speculation before he knew what he should have to pay for it himself. Afterward he succeeded in buying it for £162,000, much below what he had anticipated. The Nizam did not object to paying Mr. Jacob what he agreed, but the English government, learning of it, interfered in the matter. The Nizam had already paid Mr. Jacob £150,000 and was to pay the second £150,000 soon, but the government would not allow him to do so. It may be that Indian rajahs with their customary extravagance have a habit of buying imperial diamonds when the money is badly needed for affairs of state. At any rate the government objected and alleged, among other things, that Mr. Jacob had hypnotized the Nizam. Of Mr. Jacob's occult powers I know nothing, though, according to an article in Borderland, the journal of the believers, they are most remarkable, and, as you know, Crawford endows him with magical qualities. The case was decided in favor of Mr. Jacob, but to get the rest of the money is another thing. He has, however, every confidence in the Nizam and thinks he will pay him.

The Nizam of Hyderabad, Mir Mahbub Ali, is the most important of the independent princes, and is said to have the finest collection of jewels in the world. He naturally wishes to add the Imperial, considered the finest diamond in the world, to the collection. The "mines of Golconda," that have come to be a proverbial expression for riches, are near Hyderabad, or rather they are not, for there is another inaccuracy dear to me

A Modern Prince of India

that has been brought to light. The jewels are not found in Golconda, but at Partial, near the frontier, and they are only cut and polished at Golconda.

Mr. Jacob had with him many remarkable jewels, remarkable oftener for size than water, for Indian princes fancy large gems. I should not be a woman if I did not love jewels, and my eyes were dazzled and delighted by the display. Some of them were worth large sums; a pigeon-blood ruby, set around with diamonds, was valued at 50,000 rupees, which divides by three for dollars, a diamond worth 30,000 rupees and others equally valuable. There was a resplendent head band intended to be worn by a rajah. It had a row of half a dozen huge emeralds set in gold. They were delicately engraved after an old fashion. In the center there was a richly jeweled clasp to hold a white aigrette, and below, just over the forehead, hung a sparkling diamond, the loveliest that I have ever seen. It was about the size of a pecan nut, and was cut with facets on all sides. It hung by a silken string, and I swung the glittering little pendant of light in my fingers, enjoying as I would enjoy fine music its sparkling radiance. There were rubies, too, as large as the end of my thumb, bundles of unset stones, strings of huge pearls, shining rows of topaz and the less precious stones, a magnificent cat's-eye, heavy arm bands set with varicolored gems, all the barbaric gorgeousness that you can imagine.

These are a few of the many things which Mr. Jacob showed to us. He is the soul of generosity and kindness. "Oh, yes, Mr. Jacob," said a gentleman to me.

One Way Round the World

"Every one knows of Mr. Jacob. He has the most charming home in the world in Simla, and he is a prince of hospitality."

If I have the good fortune to visit India again, I shall care most to renew acquaintance with this unique and interesting personage.

. . . .

The first thing to learn about Delhi is that it is pronounced Delee, not Delhie, as the uncompromising Indiana accent has it. After you have learned that you may start out to see the sights.

Our frailties, foibles and fads are all understood in the Chandni Chowk, or Silver street, if they are not elsewhere. The Chandni Chowk is the street of the dealers in sandal wood, ivory, silver, Indian jewelry, embroidery in gold and silver threads, ivory miniatures, Kashmir shawls, enamels, rugs, pottery, metal work, all the host of articles that are manufactured in India, and sold, no doubt, chiefly to foreigners. The shops of the Chandni Chowk are not small native establishments, but are built, if I may so express it, on the European plan. No such lively "catch-as-catch-can" shopping, however, goes on in any place in Europe. As soon as you enter the street you are swooped down on by a horde of screaming individuals, who shout the praises of their masters' goods and revile the articles of their competitors. They make life miserable for you all the time in Delhi, and if you are ever indiscreet enough to let them know that you fancy a thing they have they will dog your

A Modern Prince of India

footsteps from morning till night, appearing at the most astonishing and unexpected moments like genii of the lamp, and producing the article from somewhere in the folds of their voluminous garments. Their entrances and exits are as mysterious as the fairy godmothers. The dealers often naively ask you whether you prefer to buy at "fixed price" or to bargain. Either way you are like clay in the hands of the potter, and he is sure to get the best of you. Cards of addresses descend on your head as thick as snowflakes, each one coming from the principal dealer in his line of goods in Delhi. If you could only be stonily indifferent to these pests all would be well, but shops are ever beguiling and those of the Chandni Chowk are no exception.

The fort in Delhi is much like the one built in Agra by Akbar the Great. There are the same massive, rich, red sandstone walls, and you enter through just such a story-book entrance, crossing a deep moat, passing through a high gate and winding in along a road enclosed by towering stone walls, where the horses' hoofbeats echo sharply. It seems an awesome thing to pierce such an impregnable fortress, and you half expect to see armed men spring up along the walls to bar your progress. Inside is the wonderful Dewan-i-Khas, or Hall of Special Audience, of which I have already told you. It is a fancy of mine not to send you a picture of the Dewan-i-Khas. The photographer's art is a wonderful one, and in some directions and cases it has been known to flatter nature, but there are times when it is too inadequate, too disappointing. Build rather in your imagination an exquisite structure of white and gold, with a tracery of precious marble and a gleam of jewels, then when you come to India you may find your vision enclosed within the massive walls of the old fort at Delhi. It is the Dewan-i-Khas of the Moguls. In the center of this Hall of Audience, on a platform of white marble once stood the famous peacock throne, the wonder of its age. Its cost has been estimated at thirty millions of dollars. The throne consisted of a canopy and chair all of solid gold, decorated lavishly with jewels. At the back of the chair was the spreading tail of a peacock in which the colors of the feathers were exactly imitated in precious stones. There is also said to have been a parrot carved from a single emerald. This wonderful piece of Mogul extravagance was finally sold by an impecunious descendant of its creator. It was necessarily sold in pieces, because of its great value, and a part of it is now in the possession of Victoria, Queen of Great Britain and Ireland and Empress of India.

Before we went away we visited another mosque. Afterward we haggled and dallied with a vendor of the pretty ivory miniatures that are painted by the bushel in Delhi. We offered him an amount which he indignantly spurned, and drove away. After we had rounded a corner we heard a shout and turned to see a flash and a flutter of turban and drapery coming full speed after us. It was Mahomet (they are all named Mahomet something or other) coming with the miniatures. He had forgotten his indignation of a few minutes before,

THE FORT AT DELHI

A Modern Prince of India

and smilingly accepted the amount that we had offered him, so smilingly that we bought them rather apprehensively. Long practice has made us skillful, however, and I don't suppose we paid more than twice what they were worth.

Another day we went out to the see the Kutab Minar, a wonderful soaring column of fluted stone that rises 238 feet above the broad plain which it overlooks. The sandstone is richly carved in bands with texts from the Koran. The carving is as perfect as in the days when it was done, 650 years ago. It is a tower of victory built by a Mohammedan conqueror, and it has looked down on an unbroken Mohammedan rule from the time it was built until the mutiny of 1857.

The road from Delhi to the Kutab Minar runs through a level stretch of country known as Old Delhi, a territory as rich in ruins and buried buildings as the Campagna near Rome. Here is another great city that time has mysteriously effaced. On every hand are the ruins of magnificent tombs which are gradually crumbling into dust. Sometimes they are surrounded to the very edge of their walls with waving green fields of wheat. Sometimes a cut through a ridge shows a wall of solid masonry over which the soil has swept like a wave. It seems like a vast inundation of earth. Old Delhi is unspeakably wonderful if one pauses to think of its long history, of its glories, of the triumphs of art and architecture over which this dust has rolled. So many spans of life have glided by since that buried wall was laid by human hands!

One Way Round the World

When we got back to New Delhi, full of life and modern dust, we dissipated our pensive mood by a tilt in the shops.

We bought some ivory and sandal wood boxes of a fixed price dealer who had the things we wanted, and he actually stuck to a good high price. The bargaining habit has grown upon me, and I find that a fixed price arrangement robs the deal of half its zest. In the little shop I was introduced to a real live prince, a brother of the King of Servia, I believe. He spoke beautiful French and was an agreeable personage generally, but I thought him a little too ready to speak of the presents he was going to make to Massenet or the Prince of Wales, and the magnificent gifts which he himself was receiving from the rajahs.

Another dusty ride in the railway brought us to Jeypore, or Jaipur, or Jeypoor, with still other variations, one of the most delightful Indian cities that we have seen. Jeypore is agreeably free from things that one ought to do and agreeably full of things that one delights to do. It is a prosperous city to begin with, and plainly shows the influence of the wise and philanthropic ruler who governs it. It was the maharajah of Jeypore, by the way, who visited the World's Fair, and he is an intelligent and advanced sovereign. There is a palace high up on the hill overlooking the city, and below it, in large letters along the hillside, is the motto "Welcome," in our own familiar English characters. The motto itself is ugly enough, but the sentiment is gracious and pleasing. One feels a genial interest in this cour-

TOMBS IN OLD DELHI

A Modern Prince of India

teous maharajah, and visits his palaces and stables and museums with an added interest.

In the maharajah's stables we saw a number of fine horses. There are three hundred and fifty satiny beauties of all breeds and colors, and there are three hundred and fifty attendants to see that these equine aristocrats are well taken care of. In the evening you can see them taking exercise in the streets, mounted by the turbaned attendants, and very often a pack of the maharajah's dogs will be out for a constitutional, yelping and frolicking from sheer good spirits.

At the Zoological Garden we saw some magnificent tigers, fierce man-eaters, that growled and jumped at the bars of their cages in a way to make the shivers run along your spine. We stopped at a former dak bungalow, which has been made over and named the Family Hotel. The inevitable juggler was there, haunting the veranda, and he did some wonderfully clever tricks. Time after time he took a handful of dry sand out of a bucket of water, and we were never able to detect the trick. He also made rupees disappear and reappear in a cup in an astonishing manner, and he afterward captured a number of our own rupees in a way that was quite as neat.

At the elephants' fighting ground, a big enclosure, where the gates are barred with heavy beams, you can see the fighting elephants, vicious fellows, whose ill-temper is cultivated, and who furnish some stirring excitement when they come to settle old scores. They are chained up in a narrow walled enclosure, and are viewed by visitors from a very respectful distance. One old warrior, who had had one tusk broken off in a fight, trumpeted loudly when we appeared, and his wicked little eyes gleamed balefully at us. We retreated precipitately to the small door by which we had entered, and made no effort to conciliate him. It was not until I had two or three brick walls between myself and his highness that I breathed securely. At the left of the fighting ground is a building with latticed windows, where the ladies of the zenana, or harem, watch the battles. These latticed-windowed apartments are seen everywhere, and on one of the principal city streets is the Hall of the Winds, a bit of the great palace, which juts out on the street and permits the ladies of the maharajah's zenana to see the passers-by and to watch the brilliant holiday processions that occasionally pass there.

The palace gardens are filled with sweet smelling flowers, and many peacocks walk around with their rich feathers glistening in the sun, while monkeys chatter in the trees. In a little lake there are some gaping crocodiles, which stretch their yawning jaws for the pieces of meat that the idlers dangle on the end of a string and pull teasingly away from them. They shut their jaws with a resounding, ominous snap that echoes across the lake. I suppose one of their brown tormentors would make a most satisfactory meal for them if he accidently tumbled in. The palace is not so beautiful, but the maharajah has chosen wisely. Instead of squandering his great income in a useless magnificence he has spent

A ZENANA CART

A Modern Prince of India

it for his people, and there is an air of smiling content everywhere in Jeypore. The streets are wide and airy, the people well dressed, the buildings imposing. Many of them have been built by the maharajah himself, and they are painted uniformly in rose color, with a tracery of white.

The large fountain square, where the four great thoroughfares converge, is as picturesque a place as you will find in a journey round the world. You never tire of it. There is always some fresh scene there to amuse, or divert, or astonish you. When the blazing Indian sun has sunk below the horizon and a fine evening breeze is blowing in from the hills, all Jeypore seems to be in the streets in holiday mood and holiday colors. Red and green and blue and orange—every vivid color known to the dyer's art—vie with one another for supremacy. The Jeypore costume is the most picturesque of India. The men wind their turbans to one side, jauntily, the women wear a quantity of full colored skirts with tinseled hems, and their heads and arms and ankles are heavy with jewelry. The sole garment of the small boy is usually a gay-colored little ulster that should come down to his heels, but it is always buttonless, and it floats in the breeze behind him as he runs. There are many groups of naked ascetics, smeared with ashes and chanting a doleful song. Sometimes there will be a nautch girl dancing in the street, surrounded by a circle of admirers.

It is a fascinating bit of oriental life, a scene that reminds one that the world is wide, and that there are many kinds of people in it. The home land seems very far away amid that smiling sea of brown faces, that alien race, that shifting, glowing crowd. A faint haze hangs over memory. One feels again that sensation of unreality, that apprehension that the panorama of the streets and the azure, **cloudless dome of** the sky is a bright-colored dream.

. . . .

After all we went to Bombay. Bombay—the **plague,** the plague—Bombay—a couple of **words that have trav**eled far and wide together of late. Small-pox in Kobe, **the cholera in Singapore** and now the plague in Bombay—a grisly trio, truly. Yet we were assured that there was little danger in passing through **the** city, so stricken with the deadly fever. To return to Calcutta would have meant a long delay, for every passage on the steamers was secured for weeks ahead, and to Bombay we went, arriving one sunny morning. We saw no evidences **of the ravages** of the pestilence, **except the** temporary houses **put up for the poor,** who **were being** removed from **the infected quarters,** and an occasional burning bungalow which the plague's black finger had touched and which **had** to be destroyed utterly. Eighty-**six new** cases and eighty-three deaths was the sinister death-roll of the day published in the morning paper. The railway station was almost deserted, and the passengers arriving with us, most of them intending **to go directly on board** the "Caledonia," as we did, had the greatest difficulty in finding **enough porters to carry** the luggage to the carriages. We scurried through the city,

A Modern Prince of India

a beautiful city, too, but deserted and forlorn for the moment, half afraid to draw a comfortable breath, and once on the P. & O. tug we were soon aboard the "Caledonia." Then we breathed at length a hope that we hadn't met any little plague bacilli out for a stroll. It reassured us somewhat to learn that three or four courageous countrymen of ours had spent several days sightseeing in Bombay without any bad results.

But the quarantine! That was the *pièce de résistance* in the way of conversation all the way to Suez. Should we be allowed to land in Egypt? Should we be allowed to land at Brindisi? Should we have to go all the way to London? What, oh what, should we not have to do? The officers of the ship were, as usual, non-committal, and rumor was rife. Nothing would be known, we were assured, until we got to Suez, but that fact did not stem the current of conjecture. At any rate, we would have to be fumigated! Here was a novelty, indeed. The Wise One said she rather liked the idea. Not every one has a chance to be fumigated on his way around the world, and, at least, we'd pay no extra baggage on germs. Meanwhile the "Caledonia" steamed swiftly onward. The weather in the Red Sea was cool and rough. Every one had warned us to remember that the Red Sea was sure to be hot. Consequently we had all our wrong things in the steamer trunks and all our right things in the hold. We blamed our friends and the weather impartially. That is always much more satisfactory than blaming one's self. The stars all glowed bright at night, and we all gave ourselves cramps in the backs of our necks gazing at the Southern Cross. Let me whisper that this famous constellation, the subject of poetic flights, was pronounced a "fake" by an unappreciative young man, who declared that it takes five stars to make a cross, instead of four, and let me whisper that I agreed with him.

The morning of the eighth day we steamed into the "roads" at Suez. To our consternation we had learned the day before we arrived at Aden that one of the first-class passengers had small-pox. They tried to land the unfortunate man at Aden, but he was refused by the health officers and was brought back to the ship and put in the hospital. We reflected that our already slim chances of landing in Egypt had probably gone down to zero. Early in the morning at Suez the quarantine authorities climbed on board and turned every one out unceremoniously in various states of dress and undress for inspection. We all tried to look as robust as possible, and now, with the hope that you have really become interested to know whether we were allowed to land or not, I'll announce that the subject will be continued in our next chapter.

XXIII

In Egypt

EARLY in the morning there was a scurry and a flurry on board the "Caledonia," and the passengers hustled unceremoniously out of bed. "We are in the roads, Miss," announced the stewardess, "and the officers are just coming on board for medical inspection." Medical inspection has ever a pompous sound and calls to mind a row of blue-uniformed and brass-buttoned individuals whose opinions are to be respected. Having sailed from plague-stricken Bombay and having a case of small-pox on board, we felt particularly vulnerable, and awaited the inspection with some anxiety. "Would passengers be allowed to land at Suez?" "Would they be allowed to land at Brindisi?" "Should we be obliged to go all the way to London and be content with this tantalizing glimpse of the shores of Egypt?" Questions and surmises and sensational reports electrified the air, as groups of people, in a greater or less state of *déshabillé*, stood around on the deck and discussed the situation.

"All of you seem fairly healthy," said the head inspector, a young giant of an Englishman, with twinkling eyes. "Think we'll let you land here, but you will have to go to Moses Wells." "Oh!" we ejaculated ruefully, for Moses Wells meant quarantine and fumigation. "If you want to get away from Egypt soon, be non-committal about where you have come from or the steamship companies may refuse to take you," was the inspector's private advice to me. "They are all in a blue funk about this plague," he continued. "Blue funk" is not in my vocabulary, but I gathered that it meant a panicky scare.

The officers gave the most of their attention to the crew, who were lined up on deck, a row of dark-skinned fellows, principally Indians. They don their best togs for inspection and some quartermaster may be arrayed in such a dazzling suit of satin and gold embroidery that you would mistake him for a rajah.

The uncertainties of what fumigation had to offer decided a good many wavering tourists that they really didn't care much whether they saw Cairo and the pyramids or not, and they continued their way to Brindisi. So, when the formalities were over, it was just a handful of people who climbed down into the little boat that lay alongside waiting for us.

No sooner were we settled than the "Caledonia's" screws began churning the water and she steamed away from us toward the town of Suez, which we could see plainly in the distance. She steamed straight into the land, apparently, for she was entering the canal, and presently we saw her masts and funnels with their trail of smoke across a stretch of yellow sand.

We were in quarantine and the P. & O. tug that usually takes passengers ashore had refused to have any-

In Egypt

thing to do with us until we had paid our respects to Moses Wells.

Over to the right we could see the oasis that bears that historic name, and at a short distance from it were the low brick buildings of the quarantine station. The oasis is not the place in the desert where Moses struck the rock, but it is said that the children of Israel halted there to get water from the wells. Our little boat sailed leisurely in that direction, aided by two rowers who pulled lazily at their creaking oars. But no one could have found it in his heart to be impatient of the slow progress. The place seemed too fair to leave. The water was heavenly blue. It mirrored the azure dome above it and flashed back the radiant glint of liquid color. This sea might be named Red at sunset when it is aflame with the sun's ruddy glow, but by day, under the clear, rainless Arabian sky, it is a wonderful, changing, shading, sparkling blue. Fluttering over the pellucid water and floating on its bosom was a great flock of gray and white gulls that flashed their wings in the sunlight and caught the bright light on the tips of them just as the wing-like sails of the fisher boats did. The distant sandy shores were a brilliant yellow and beyond them rose the gaunt mountains of the desert. Their bare slopes are cheerless enough, but they were glorified by the soft violet haze that hung over them, a rich unmistakable violet that is rare in nature. Indeed, the coloring of Egyptian landscapes is unique and the Nile sunsets are one of Egypt's glories.

At Moses Wells we were greeted by an agreeable

One Way Round the World

French doctor and a buxom Madame of enormous proportions, who didn't look as if she had ever had any of the ills that the flesh is heir to. Even the quarantine victims are welcome in that lonely place, and we did our best to dissipate the depressing pall that hung over it. The fumigation was mild. Our steamer rugs and chairs and some of our clothing were put in a big boiler and royally steamed for twenty-five minutes, but we ourselves escaped. A glimpse of the little square boxes of rooms, furnished with mysterious faucets and pipes and a small wooden chair for the fumigatee had not tended to reassure us, so we omitted the experience gratefully.

Our men were waiting to take us to Suez in the small boat. One of them saw the ukulele in my hand, the little instrument, you remember, that has shared my fortunes ever since we left Honolulu. He leaned toward me with an engaging smile. "Lady," he said, "make a dance." So I played for him a little, to his evident delight, and to the neglect of his duties as an oarsman. It was finally found necessary to politely recall to his attention that we wanted to get the 3 o'clock train for Cairo. He rose smilingly and spoke to the rest of the crew in Arabic. They began to pull at the oars, at the same time chanting a musical refrain. "What do you sing?" I asked. "I sing to the north wind," he replied. "I sing Blow, North Wind, Blow!" But we were not destined to receive a proof of the north wind's amiability or lack of it, for in another quarter of an hour the P. & O. launch had picked us up and it carried

In Egypt

us swiftly to Suez. At the entrance of the canal we saw the stars and stripes floating in the breeze over the American Consulate, and that sight is always marked as an event by the wanderer from home.

Lo! we were in the land of still another style of head-gear. The fez, this time, red and jaunty, was everywhere in evidence as well as the white and vari-colored turbans of the Arabs. We showered blessings on the fez of one small Turk, an urchin who came walking by the car window with a basket of hot hard-boiled eggs. There had been no time for lunch, and those eggs, with dessert of sweet Jaffa oranges, saved the day. The gratification was mutual, and our small boy skipped away jingling a goodly number of piasters in his pocket. Probably he had made the sale of a lifetime. We tried, too, some coffee *à la Turque*, which was handed in through the car window. It is a Turkish mixture of coffee grounds, sugar and hot water, and is served in tiny cups.

The railway follows the canal, running through the desert between fields of barren sand. Occasionally, where irrigation was possible, a little green was growing and almond trees were blossoming. When one looks at that desolate waste, one realizes under what difficulties the great canal was built and the immensity of De Lessep's achievement. The sun set splendidly, and when it was gone the white moonlight turned the sand fields into snow. Occasionally we would see the starry cluster of lights on a big steamer that was moving slowly through the canal. We dined at Ismailia

One Way Round the World

and at Ismailia the Wise One and Paterfamilias completed their journey around the globe. Just two years before they had dined at Ismailia and started westward. This time they had come from the east. To put a girdle around the earth makes it seem rather smaller they agreed. Late that night we arrived in Cairo and were soon fast asleep in that famous and most delightful of hostelries—Shepheard's Hotel. No wonder that after our Indian experience it seemed to us palatial, or that after that long day we slept well.

. . . .

Cairo, the gay, the cosmopolitan! There is an endless fascination in the quixotic stream of people that fills the streets. French, Italian, English, Greek, Turkish, and I know not how many other languages are seen everywhere on the signs, and men of all nationalities rub elbows in the sauntering crowd. You could idle away days sitting on the broad veranda at Shepheard's, watching the passersby. It is said, by the way, that this famous old hotel has had more notable people under its roof than any other in the world. In the afternoon the veranda is crowded with a bevy of fashionable idlers who chatter and sip tea. Perhaps a chic Parisienne, in the most extreme and modish of frocks, is sitting near a dashing American girl, who has for a neighbor again a fresh-skinned, blue-eyed Fraülein, or a stately Russian. In the street a harem cart, a sort of diminutive dray, is passing. It is drawn by an ornately decorated donkey who jingles with bells, and on the cart are sitting four or five or six black shrouded women, the ladies of a

In Egypt

harem out for an airing. They are swathed in drapery until every line of the figure is concealed. Between the eyes, running up and down the nose and resting on the forehead, is a peculiar piece of metal much like a spool, which holds the heavy black veil that conceals all of the face except the eyes and forehead. I do not think they fall in love at first sight in Cairo. The large, dark eyes of the women, rimmed with black cosmetic, have a somber, listless expression, and I never caught a gleam of merriment in them. These women are as far removed from their sisters of the veranda as they well could be. The orient and the occident do not bring together blending conditions but sharp contrasts. Another type of woman is to be seen in the elegantly dressed wives of the rich Turks who whirl by in their modern carriages, drawn by spirited horses, giving one a glimpse of gold embroidered garments and head dresses and the filmy folds of a white yashmak, that has a touch of coquetry about it, for it only half conceals the face and has not the hideous spool of metal to distort the eyes.

Flying ahead of these equipages are the most picturesque of all the picturesque figures in Cairo, the sais, or runners, who clear the way for the carriages of the rich. I say flying because their light tread seems too airy to describe otherwise. They run for hours ahead of the horses, touching the ground so lightly with their toes, as they speed along, that it seems they must be Oriental Mercuries with a pair of wings concealed in their turbans to keep them poised. They are armed with long, graceful wands, which carry out the illusion. Their shapely, muscular legs are bare and they wear baggy trousers and full sleeves made of a thin white material that is always spotless. The costume is rendered elegant by a jacket richly braided in gold, wound at the waist with a plaid silk scarf. A bit of red on the arm and in the turban, gives the final brilliant touch. One evening as we drove out to the Ghezireh Palace Hotel, we came upon a group of sais who had been left by their masters to rest until they returned, for the boulevard is broad and the sais were not needed. There were a score or more of them, and as they stood laughing and chatting together they made a picture that I have not seen surpassed for picturesqueness on my way around the globe.

After the carriages with their resplendent sais have passed the next passenger by the highway is apt to be a solemn camel, lurching slowly along on his way, or a jingling donkey mounted by a long-limbed rider whose feet almost touch the ground. The donkey is prodded and poked by a donkey boy, so-called, who trots along behind him and bestows many an idle whack that isn't needed, as well as many that are. The donkey boy may be a graybeard and a grandfather, but he is known as a boy to the end of his days. He wears a long, loose coat, usually of an indigo-blue stuff, sometimes of colored stripes, and a white turban. The costume of the well-to-do Arabs is very handsome. They are large, finely formed men, as a rule, and the long, flowing broadcloth coats, richly lined and braided, suit them admirably.

SAIS

In Egypt

Their dignity of garb, combined with a marked dignity of manner and gesture, make them the imposing figures of the streets.

One day we secured the services of a dragoman, as the guide is called in Egypt. He was an intelligent, handsome fellow, and had evidently omitted none of his opportunities for extracting extra piasters from the tourist's pocketbook, for he was very well dressed. On his head he wore a fez of a satiny quality of felt. His coat was beautifully embroidered. Around his neck he had wound a brilliant silk scarf, and his feet were encased in sky-blue slippers. He bowed and greeted us in very good English, and we soon departed at his suggestion for a round of sightseeing. Unless you are to sojourn in Cairo for many a month, you can not consign your duties to the far-away to-morrow as the Arab does, and plan to idly happen on all the things there are to see. Neither can you model your conduct by the Egyptians. When you are in Egypt, do as the Egyptians do, would be idle advice. A diligent search through all that maze of nationalities would fail to unearth a class or a race that is known as Egyptian. The nation that built the pyramids erected monuments which have long outlived itself. The Copts are supposed to be the only descendants of the ancient Egyptians. The kinky-haired, ebony-skinned Nubians and Soudanese are frequently seen in Cairo. The Soudanese are staunch fighters, and are giving her majesty's troops no end of trouble in the Soudan.

Piloted by Mahomet Shokrey Pilley, which was the

hybrid name of our dragoman, we alighted first at an empty, open platform overlooking an arm of the Nile. Below, in the river, were some dahabeahs, the graceful river craft of this noble stream, and a busy, shouting, gesticulating crowd was unloading freight and disposing of it. On the opposite bank were some tumble-down palaces, and beyond, between rows of waving date palms, we had the first view of the great pyramids, two toy-like peaks that notched the rim of the horizon. On this platform there is a yearly festival, when the figure of a woman, dressed in silks and decorated with gewgaws, is thrown into the Nile as an offering to the river god. In the old days a human sacrifice of a beautiful maiden (in stories of this sort the maiden should by all means be beautiful) was always made, but when the Mohammedans entered Egypt a protest was sent to the caliph at Mecca and the sacrifice was forbidden. George Eber's story, "The Bride of the Nile," has this old-time custom for its theme. The ceremony still continues, and the khedive attends.

The khedive is seen driving in the streets almost every day. His coming is announced by a blast of bugles and a clatter of outriders, and every one turns to see the procession go by. The khedive is a stout, dark young man, who wears a fez and a suit of European clothes. It seems to me that he might have changed places with his coachman, for a diversion, without any one being the wiser. What's in a fez? No distinction, apparently, for all sorts and conditions of men wear them. The khedive touches his hand mechanically to his head, look-

BACKSHEESH. "LEDDY"

In Egypt

ing neither to the right nor to the left, and continues his conversation with his companion.

After we left the platform we visited the island of Roda to see the Nilometer, an ancient pillar carved with Cufic inscriptions from the Koran. The pillar stands in a walled enclosure, a sort of well so arranged that the river water can enter and show the level of the Nile. In the old days the taxes were levied each year according to the rise of the river. On this island Mahomet showed us the spot where Pharaoh's daughter found Moses in the bullrushes. There is nothing but a wall of brick and cement there now, and no sign of rushes, but I've no doubt that Mahomet would tell you which way the wind was blowing at the time, or in which direction Moses' head lay, if you cared to know.

We wandered in the shady gardens on the island and gazed curiously at the latticed windows of a palace for a harem. I can not explain the mysterious attraction that this institution has for the western mind, but I observe that at the mere mention of the word people prick up their ears and grow attentive. As we walked out of the shady garden into the glaring sun, the keeper of the gate held out his hand for backsheesh, that pestiferous backsheesh that rings in your ears from morning till night and haunts your dreams. Being rewarded with a small silver coin, because there were no coppers at hand, he smiled and expressed his gratitude volubly. "What does he say?" we inquired of Mahomet. "He prays Allah to bless you," replied Mahomet, "and guide you safely to your far-away land." The wish was graceful, but it rather spoiled the effect to know that he would have consigned us with a curse to the remotest corner of an undesirable region if he had received a fee that he considered small.

If one had two lives to live, there would be time to study Arabic for the sake of its highly poetical expressions. One day we were sitting near the fountain in the court of the mosque of Mahomet Ali in the Citadel, a beautiful structure of alabaster, crowned by two tall, slender minarets that overlook the city far below, and can be seen for miles in every direction, even far out on the desert. "You see the man kneeling at his prayer?" said the dragoman. "I tell you what he is saying. First he wash his hands three times at the fountain. 'O Allah, I extol thee and beseech thee to keep all devils from my soul,' he say. Then he wash the mouth three times. 'O Allah, I extol thee and beseech thee to make the speeches of my mouth sweet and perfumed.' Then he wash the nostrils three times. 'O Allah, I extol thee and beseech thee to let me smell all the perfumes of Paradise.' Then his face three time. 'O Allah, I extol thee and beseech thee to make my face spotless and white on the day of judgment.' Then he wash the right forearm and he say, 'O Allah, I extol thee and beseech thee to give me the Book (the Koran) in the right hand, instead of the left.' Then he dip finger in the water and wet head three times. 'O Allah, I extol thee and beseech thee to protect my head from my enemy's sword.' Then last he wash right leg and say, 'O Allah, I extol thee and beseech thee to give me lusty strength to make the great pilgrimage (to Mecca) on foot. Thanks be to Allah in the name of the Prophet Mahomet. I believe that there is but one Allah, and Saidnah Mahomet is his messenger.'"

By this time the man we were watching had finished his ablutions, and we rose and followed him into the mosque, whose great width and height and breadth give it a wonderful solemnity and majesty. The light was dim, and the lofty ceiling of the temple seemed marvelously high over our heads. Before the tomb of Mahomet Ali some twinkling lights were burning. "You are a Mahometan, aren't you?" I inquired softly of our Mahomet. "Yes, thank God!" he replied loudly, with such unexpected fervency and satisfaction that I almost smiled. Waste none of your sympathy on the misguided heathen.

It was in the Citadel that the Mamelukes were killed by Mahomet Ali, who lies sleeping so near the scene of blood. The present dynasty has run only through seven generations, beginning with Mahomet Ali, and before that the rulers of Egypt were caliphs sent from Mecca. Just who the Mamelukes were I am not sure, a band of usurpers, probably, at any rate they were singularly unfortunate about their heads. Mahomet Ali, considering it advisable to have them all out of the way, invited them to a grand banquet at the Citadel and laid a plot to kill them all. He very nearly succeeded, for only one, Emin Bey, escaped by a perilous leap on his horse from the high Citadel wall. The place pointed out is a dizzy height from which it seems impossible to escape being dashed to pieces. But, though his horse was killed, Emin Bey reached the ground alive. Years before, the Caliph Sultan Hassan killed another band of Mamelukes, under similar circumstances, in the mosque that bears his name.

Returning from a pilgrimage to Mecca he found that a conspiracy had been formed against him by the Mamelukes, and he, too, decided that the most effective way of disposing of them was to destroy them root and branch. He succeeded in assembling them in the mosque and had them all killed. The mosque is now a majestic ruin, but the dark bloodstains of the murdered men are pointed out on the stone floor. The tombs of the Mamelukes and of the caliphs lie in a barren waste of sand outside the city, and a band of miserable outcasts find shelter within their walls. The dust blows in whirlwinds around them and I have the clearest recollection, I find, of the interminable winding and twisting, stone-walled, dusty lanes through which we drove to get to them. They are almost in ruins, but some of the domes with their delicate carvings in arabesques are unharmed and beautiful.

The Amer Mosque is curious, though there is nothing beautiful about its crumbling pillars and dilapidated court. There is a stone pillar which is said to have flown there from Mecca when struck by Mahomet's whip and told to do so. A grain in the marble shows the curl of the lash and outlines the word Allah in Arabic characters. In another place there is a rough stone which has been licked by the faithful until it is

In Egypt

covered with blood. In still another place are two marble pillars worn smooth by the brushing garments of believers. The pillars are set very close together and those who succeed in squeezing through are supposed to be sure of entering heaven.

The tomb of Ibraim Pasha, that noble old warrior who might have carried all before him if the powers had not united against him, is interesting, as are many other mosque tombs too numerous to mention. One of them is an amusing illustration of the old saw:

"When a woman will she will and you may depend on it,
And when she won't she won't and that's the end on it."

The khedivia, mother of the present khedive, became queen regent on the sudden death of her husband, and as such she insisted upon having her husband buried with her family instead of laying him beside his ancestors where the line of khedives is buried. She carried her point, too, by threatening suicide if thwarted, and Tewfick Pasha now lies besides his wife's mother in a beautiful little mosque tomb erected by the khedivia. It is still unfinished and she goes there to watch the progress of the work. The floor is carpeted with rare oriental rugs that are a delight to the eye, a real chromatic luxury, and the walls are being frescoed in a harmony of rich color and gold. A number of youths were sitting on their heels near the entrance, with the little folding stand that holds the Koran open before them, swaying their bodies and droning passages from the Holy Book. The Mahometan's education prac-

One Way Round the World

tically begins and ends with the Koran, and it is funny to see a roomful of little boys at school, each sitting on the floor with his Koran stand in front of him, each yelling his lesson at the top of his voice. If he becomes momentarily drowsy or forgetful the teacher taps him with a stick and he starts in again vigorously.

It seems strange in this eastern setting that suggests the Arabian Nights at every turn to find interwoven the thread of familiar Christian history and to have pointed out, on descending a dark and steep stone staircase in an old Coptic chapel, some underground apartments that are said to be the rooms of the inn in which Mary and Joseph stopped during the flight into Egypt. There are niches in the wall marked with crosses where Joseph and Mary sat with the Christ child.

XXIV

In the Shadow of the Pyramids

MARCH 17.—"Another delightful day, the joyous recollections of which are tempered by numerous flea bites and a wealth of sore muscles," says my journal. Dust, flies and fleas in Egypt form a triple alliance against comfort that I have never seen equaled. The subject of fleas has always seemed a trifle indelicate elsewhere. Not so in the land of the Pharaohs. You may launch the curse of Rome at this lively insect to an appreciative and sympathetic audience at any time. His presence is a daily reminder that the wise man builds his house upon a rock, far away from sand. The flies, too, are attentive and sticky. They refuse to move unless actually brushed off, and the boys on the streets have small rush fly brushes for sale. We experienced, too, a real sand-storm. The wind blew a gale, and the air was filled with a great, yellowish haze. We shut ourselves indoors and watched the sand beat and dash against the window pane just as a heavy rain does. Then when the wind died down, the sand either whisked back to the desert on a last favorable breeze or settled down into the dusty streets, and we were back in the sunny, serene Cairo of ordinary days.

One Way Round the World

The morning of the 17th we departed early in the morning for a visit to Sakhara and the buried city of Memphis. It is several hours' journey up the Nile to them, and the trip gives a very good idea, so those who know say, of the whole Nile trip. One can not have a favorable season everywhere in a flying trip around the world, and we were too late in Egypt to go up the Nile. We took that morning, as everybody takes, one of the Cook boats, the Tewfick. Thomas Cook & Son, the tourists' agents, are omnipresent, and no where more in evidence than on the Nile, where they own all the best boats and can make much more satisfactory arrangements with the wily Arab than any uninitiated person can.

The great river of Egypt is a beautiful stream of lordly breadth, even in the dry season. After Cairo is passed and the lofty tapering minarets of the mosque of Mahomet Ali have finally faded from view, the river is bordered by two strips of green and fertile fields, the scant territory that can be cultivated by irrigation, and beyond lies the waste of sand that marks the beginning of the desert. It was one of many surprises to me to learn that the desert, so burning hot by day, is cool and comfortable at night. The sand radiates the heat as quickly as it absorbs it, and for a cool evening drive people leave the city and go toward the desert. I was told that there are places where the sand is hot enough in daytime to roast an egg, but where a thin layer of ice has frozen at night. That sounds a little too much like the tales of a celebrated Baron to be credited, but of

In the Shadow of the Pyramids

one thing I can assure you. If you live in Indiana the year round you need be afraid of no extremes of temperature anywhere. It was cooler on the equator than it is on some of our July afternoons, and I am told that in Siberia the mercury doesn't sink much further out of sight than it does with us in winter.

But to resume. The villages along the Nile are dusty, tumble-down, deserted-looking collections of houses surrounded by a cluster of feather duster date-palms. At the landing a crowd of donkey boys was waiting for the party, and the dragoman warned us not to attempt to land before the "fight," meaning the selection of donkeys and donkey boys. So we leaned against the rail of the Tewfick and watched the scrimmage. In his mildest conversation the Arab seems ready at any moment to come to blows, and when there really is cause for a discussion, his extra gymnastics and flow of language are most diverting. The poor donkeys received a good many extra whacks in the excitement, and our dragoman succeeded in extracting three very good little animals from the *mêlée* for us.

"He name Yankee Doodle," said Hassan, my donkey boy, who really was a boy, a coarse, ugly, good-natured urchin of twelve or fifteen. He had made a good guess when he said that the donkey's name was Yankee Doodle. If his sharp eyes had detected an English cast to my frock or my features he would have said that the donkey's name was Prince of Wales. Hassan trotted along all day behind my steed and assured me many times that I had a good donkey, that he was a good donkey boy and that I was a good lady. These boys pick up a few phrases of half a dozen languages, and when their list of amenities is exhausted they gleefully begin over again. By dint of many threats of no backsheesh I succeeded in keeping Hassan from belaboring Yankee Doodle and he trotted along all those weary hot miles patiently and easily. I feel much indebted to him for his docility and perseverance, but I can not bring myself to approve of his preference for the extreme outside edge of banks and uncertain paths.

Our route lay in a circle which took us to many ruins and historic places of interest, unearthed by the Egyptologists. We stopped first to see two statues. The huge one of Rameses II has suffered the indignity of being stretched flat on his back and having a galvanized iron roof put over him. But the desecration par excellence is the iron bridge that has been built across his royal chest so that people may study his proportions from above. The second place we visited was the tomb of Mena, where we went through many underground chambers and passages and waved candles along the walls to see the delicately carved inscriptions in hieroglyphics and the rows of queer little Egyptian men and women that parade endlessly along these deserted halls. The books will tell you pages about the absence of perspective in Egyptian drawings and sculpture and quite mix you up by their deductions of whys and wherefores. To my untutored artistic sense these little companies of youths and maidens looked as if they had been run through a wringer and neatly pasted to the background.

DAHABEAHS ON THE NILE

In the Shadow of the Pyramids

The ruins have all been almost, if not quite, engulfed by the shifting sand, and you would pass the ruins of the city of Memphis without knowing they were there if they were not pointed out to you. The wonderful Serapeum, which contains the sarcophagi of the sacred bulls, is now completely under ground. One gropes along the dark, hot corridors, peering into the adjacent chambers to see the sarcophagi, with their granite covers awry and broken, which once held the mummies of the sacred bulls. It was with the greatest difficulty that these covers were lifted by modern engineers, and how the ponderous sarcophagi were handled and placed there remains a mystery.

Again we pursued our way on donkeyback, passing the "step" pyramid of Sakhara. It stands back in the desert proper, and is surrounded by rolling hills of rich, gold-colored sand. A glimpse of the fertile valley far away toward the river makes its desolate loneliness all the more striking. As our little party filed back to the landing the sun was setting. It flamed in the sky and burnished the water. The whole landscape was aglow. We watched its glory slowly fade as we steamed regretfully back to Cairo.

. . . .

"This morning to the Ghizeh Museum," said the Wise One, so we gracefully acquiesced and drove out along the shady Ghizeh road, with its rows of lebbec trees, to visit the great museum of the world for Egyptian antiquities. There is ever a stream of oriental passers-by on this road, many black-veiled women and gayly-dressed men, hosts of donkeys and line after line of camels, loaded with sweet-smelling clover, such heavy burdens of it that you might think the country was coming to town. The museum is a handsome building, which contains a collection of antiquities that it would take months to see and study. Either a life-time or a morning might be satisfactorily devoted to it, and we chose the latter. We were much interested in the queer little mummies of cats and dogs, fish and crocodiles, as well as in the mummies of the various Rameses. It is just as well that mummifying is a lost art, and it is to be hoped that no one is spending his time looking for it. Why not let the body moulder into dust, instead of keeping it in such a ghastly resemblance of what it was in life; and how dreadful to put the kingly body of Rameses the Great into a glass case in a museum to be stared at by every idle visitor. Near the mummy cases there is a wooden statue, supposed to be the oldest in existence, of a benignant, fat old man, and some interesting stones bearing the same inscription in three languages—hieroglyphics, Cufic and Greek. The most famous of these valuable stones, the Rosetta, is in the British Museum, but several that were equally useful in deciphering hieroglyphics are in Cairo. After these keys were discovered it was found to be a comparatively easy task to decipher the hieroglyphic inscriptions. A member of a certain party which lately traveled in Egypt, who is something of a practical joker, attracted a great deal of attention as well as admiration

In the Shadow of the Pyramids

to himself by reading the inscriptions to a circle of attentive listeners whenever there was an opportunity. He was ingenious and had a lively imagination, and, so far as I know, nobody ever discovered that he didn't know one character from another.

The jewelry in the museum is curious and effective in design, and much of it shows an astonishing knowledge of the goldsmith's art and of enamels. We stopped as we came away in the sales-room connected with the museum, where antiquities are for sale at modern, if not moderate, prices. The favorites are the scarab seals, carved with the beetle, emblem of immortality, on one side, and an inscription intended for a seal on the other. They are found in the mummy cases, and the museum is the only place where one can be sure of getting the genuine article. Real antiques are now manufactured by the bushel in Cairo. Cloisonné in Japan, brocades in China, gems in Ceylon, ivories in India, scarabs in Egypt! Unless you are an abnormal being, you succumb to the fascination of each in its turn.

I was surprised to find that a mummy can be bought for as modest a sum as thirty dollars—not a mummy of a Pharaoh, to be sure, at that price, but a guaranteed specimen. Mummies, let me whisper, must be bought with the same care as scarabs, for there are modern mummies as well in the market.

. . . .

Everybody drives in the Mousky, that quaint street in Cairo that has been so faithfully copied and set down in several foreign lands, even carrying the atmosphere of the lazy East to as alien a spot as Chicago; everybody wanders in the brilliant, crowded oriental bazars, and everybody climbs the pyramids, everybody who can. Old Cheops can not be ascended in a desultory manner. It takes grit and determination, to say nothing of strength and a supply of fortitude beside, to endure the twinges of protesting muscles for a good many days afterwards. One salient point in the achievement is that you only need enough determination to get to the top. You must get down.

'Oh!" gasped our friend, Mr. K., as with a last supreme effort he pulled himself up on the small, square platform that is now the top of the pyramid, and firmly grasped the flagstaff that has been put up to show the original height of the monument. "Oh! I wouldn't have missed coming up here for a hundred dollars—and I'd give a thousand to be down!"

A view of the edge of the pyramid shows how rough and high the stones are, and what an insecure footing some of them offer. There are two Bedouins to pull and one to push, so the mounting is, if anything, easier than the coming down, when the sight of your long, precipitous path to the ground is apt to make your steps uncertain. The climb is well worth while, however, for in no other way can you get a correct idea of the immensity of these wonderful piles of stone. The pyramids are owned by the Bedouins, a race of nomads, whose tents are seen scattered around over the desert, and they charge a fee for mounting and a fee for their services. The old sheik of the Bedouins is now near

CAIRO FROM THE CITADEL

In the Shadow of the Pyramids

death, and his eldest son, who went up with us, frankly expressed the unfilial wish that his father would soon die and leave him in authority. "He too old," he said.

I am afraid I was not in a becoming frame of mind that day, for as I stood at that lofty height I did not feel the swing of the ages, as some impressionable people say they do, nor was I impressed with an awesome sense of the antiquity of these monuments of the desert. Instead, I let the sheik's son tell my fortune by a mystic circle that he drew in sand. Afterward my three pilots amused me by giving three cheers for the American young lady. I am afraid it was a desecration of Cheops' tomb.

There is something in the clear Egyptian air that fills one with a keen sense of the joy of living instead of a gentle melancholy for a dead past. The thought, however, of how many suns have risen and set on that stupendous pile makes one's span of life seem a very small link in the endless chain of time.

The view from the top of the pyramid is much the same as from Sakhara. Again you see the waves of rich warm-colored sand that roll away to the horizon in one direction and swirl around the base of the pyramids themselves. Toward the Nile, green fields and palms, and beyond, rising from the cluster of flat-roofed buff buildings of Cairo, are the minarets of the mosque of Mahomet Ali. Cairo is a city of mosques, and the graceful towers on which the muezzins mount to call the faithful to prayer are to be seen at almost every turn of the narrow streets. They are the continual delight of the amateur photographer, who draws in his mind's eye a line around everything he sees and imagines how it will look printed and mounted, and who sees in the picture before him—the busy street with its donkey riders and pedestrians, the row of bazars and their picturesque proprietors, and finally the towering minaret for a background, an ideal snap-shot.

After we had left the pyramid I mounted one of the antique moth-eaten camels that was standing near, "the ship of the desert," as he is called. He knelt for me to mount and then arose in sections, with a series of lurches and rolls that quite carried out the simile. We wended our way down into a hollow at the back of the pyramid of Cheops and soon came upon the Sphinx. This creature of mystery, with its inscrutable battered face and strange animal body, is supposed to have stood there longer than the great pyramid. Near by are the ruins of a massive temple which is thought to have been dedicated to its worship. Lying as it does in a hollow, where it was carved from the natural rock of a cliff, its proportions are not imposing and one can easily be disappointed in the first impression of it. That is lost as one studies it, and there is an undeniable fascination about it that takes one there again and again. The more one sees it, the more unfamiliar it seems to grow, and that is quite in keeping with mystery and fascination.

The dancing dervishes are another of the curious sights of Cairo. They dance at a convenient hour for themselves, probably, but at an inconveniently early

A FAIR CAIRENE

In the Shadow of the Pyramids

hour of the afternoon for visitors. Every Friday there is an early lunch at Shepheard's for those who want to go to see them. We lunched with a large and lively party of Germans and a sprinkling of other nationalities. Soon after we were all off, in a line of carriages, all on dancing dervishes intent. Driving through the busy winding streets we alighted at the opening of a passage way, and after several more circuitous turns we were ushered by our dragoman into a shabby sort of mosque. It was a circular building with a round wooden dome. Around the upper gallery was a closely latticed screen to conceal the ladies of the harem. On the lower floor a circular space was enclosed by a low wooden railing, leaving an outside aisle all around where the visitors stood. It struck me that the arrangement corresponded to my idea of a prize ring. Paterfamilias, while loth to appear well informed on the subject, explained that prize rings are usually square. After a while a procession of dervishes filed slowly in, and seated themselves on their heels in a semi-circle on the floor. They wore long, dark tunics, and each had an exaggerated elongated fez on his head. The fezes were of a nondescript woolen color and the high priest or sheik had a band of green around his. Only the descendants of Mahomet are allowed to wear the green. The pilgrimage to Mecca is always made in white. I like to think of that great white company which ever toils toward the holy city. The white is spotted and stained, no doubt, as their lives are spotted and stained, but there is an ideal purity suggested that is beautiful.

One Way Round the World

The dervishes bowed low to the ground three times and, high up in a balcony, a nasal, quavering voice began to sing from the Koran. The singer seemed to suffer a great deal so we were glad when his part of the performance was changed for a gentle drumming and weird, flutelike melody that flowed up and down a peculiar scale of unaccustomed intervals. The dervishes arose and walked solemnly three times around the circle, bowing low as they passed the sheik and kissing his hand. They then made a profound bow to one another and at a signal quickly threw off their dark tunics. They were dressed in white and wore wide bell-shaped skirts. Their feet were bare. When they began to dance they extended their arms and spun around and around till the wide skirts stood out straight and made the weird dancers look like tops. They apparently can spin endlessly, for we watched them turning for a full half hour and then left them, still whirling, to go to see the howling dervishes who began their performance a little later.

At the next place we saw another set of long-haired fanatics who were going through with their repulsive devotions. They were standing on a square raised platform in the open air. Above their heads there was a trellis of grapevines. They looked like bacchanalian revellers or a band of lunatics as they jerked up and down, with a rhythmic swing, grunting and puffing and snorting, till the noise sounded as though it came from a steam engine. It was a strange unintelligible sight.

As I looked over the crowd I saw a queer mixture of garbs. There were modish hats and frocks from Paris

In the Shadow of the Pyramids

that adorned the heads of pretty French women and Americans, good, sensible and ugly walking hats that shaded the rosy cheeks of German fraüleins. Near me were standing my two tall friends from the Argentine Republic and over on the other side I could see the black box hat of a priest of the Greek Church and the rolling brims of two Catholic priests from Rome. There were many fezes and an occasional turban of the black Soudanese boys, with scarred cheeks, who were selling fly brushes. They consider a row of scarred lines on the cheek decorative. In one corner a man was taking pictures of the scene for the cinemetograph. There was a chatter of French, and German, and English, and Spanish, and Arabic in the air. The dervishes apparently did not deem the hub-bub irreverent and finally one of them came around with the fez and took up a collection. It was then that I had a lurking suspicion that the performance of the dervishes is one of the stock sights that are kept up in all lands for the benefit of the guileless traveler who visits them and ponders over them and thinks he is seeing the life of the people. "What an odd show!" said an English woman as she walked away, and that was the best comment, on the whole, that I heard.

XXV

Due West Again

WE were to go from Ismailia to Marseilles on the Chusan, our old friend the Chusan, that had carried us from Colombo to Calcutta, and was now on her way back to London. Accordingly we took the afternoon train to Ismailia, and were soon comfortably established in the Victoria Hotel, plump against the Suez canal, plump against a little lake, rather, which just in that place forms a part of the artificial water-way from sea to sea. The Chusan was expected that evening and we learned by telegraph that she had entered the canal at Suez, so it would be a matter of only a few hours until she arrived.

We had left Cairo in the teeth of a wind storm, with the dust flying in clouds, and that night the gale rose to a hurricane. The Chusan came not. Word was sent that the storm was so severe that she was tied up in the canal and it was uncertain when she would be able to leave. There was danger of her being blown aground. The little company of fourteen who intended to get on board went reluctantly to bed. Next morning the relentless wind was still blowing fiercely and the sand dashing against the window

Due West Again

panes. The long day wore away, with occasional contradictory reports of the Chusan's plan of action or inaction, and evening and night came. Finally, at half past twelve, we were allowed to go to bed with the assurance that the ship would not come along until morning. Alas, for the mutability of human affairs! Hardly were we well asleep when there came a resounding rat-tat at our chamber doors and an irritating hoarse voice called out that the Chusan was approaching.

1:30 A. M.! It was a sleepy party that assembled in the office below and each man, as he paid his bill, took occasion to soundly berate a blonde and impassive hotel clerk for letting us go to bed, each insinuating broadly that we weren't told that the ship was about to arrive, so that the hotel might capture the shillings for a night's lodging from fourteen victims. The clerk took the matter calmly and urbanely, the shillings as well. I suppose he is accustomed to scathing remarks from sleepy guests early in the morning.

A tug was lying at the dock to take us out to the steamer. The night was clear and cold. It was bright moonlight. While we steamed around in the lake to while away the time of waiting, we could see the searchlight on the mast of the Chusan casting its great piercing shaft across the sky. Finally she steamed into the lake, we ran alongside and climbed aboard.

There were hot coffee and biscuits awaiting us in the saloon which we duly appreciated. All our troubles over, we gayly chatted and laughed over our experiences. I reflect that we probably waked every one in that part of the ship with our hilarity. If we did, I can cross off the list as balanced, one of the many times that I've been waked myself by other people's fun. The only chance of evening up such scores is to take it out on the general public.

When our luncheon was finished, the sun was rising, we had left the lake and were again slowly steaming between the narrow walls of the canal. The ships run very slowly to prevent washing the banks, and we were several hours going the short distance from Ismailia to Port Said. The monotony of the waste of desert flats was relieved by passing an occasional steamer, bound in the opposite direction.

Port Said was queer and heterogeneous. There are a quantity of little shops in the place, filled with merchandise from every quarter of the globe, and in the old days, before the visitation of the tourist, rare and lovely things could be picked up for a very small sum. Nowadays a great deal of the goods, especially the embroideries, is cheap and inferior, not to be desired at any price and showing a lamentable degeneracy in choice and combinations of color. It is unfortunate that competition and the wider opening of trade is destroying the taste for a fine fabric. With our changing fashions a comparatively cheap class of goods is imperative. What a pity that we can not find it practical to buy fabrics at twenty, thirty and forty dollars a yard, woven to be things of beauty and joys forever.

It was in Port Said that we saw the last Indian jug-

SUEZ CANAL

Due West Again

gler, who pulled the head off of one little fluffy yellow chicken and made him into two, indefinitely.

· · · · · · · ·

It was just about this time that Paterfamilias and the Wise One and I decided that we had had considerably more than a headful of sights. "There's no place like home," said the Wise One, and we assented. The Wise One's remarks, whether original or quoted, are always sure to be considered carefully and unfailingly approved.

So it happened that in the last of our journey around the world events trod fast on one another's heels.

The fair and fickle Mediterranean was on her good behavior and we had a most favorable passage to Marseilles. The sea flashed back as clear a blue to the sky as it spread over her and in that azure setting I have a remembrance of a heavenly vision, the long, lofty, snow-crowned range of mountains on the Island of Crete, which burst on our view one sunny morning. We were too far away from the island to see human habitations and the mountains hung between sea and sky as solemn, as inscrutable, as grandly beautiful as the snowy range of the Himalayas. At their feet the water was dotted with men-of-war, such tiny craft in the distance, that they looked like toys. We remembered that there was strife and bloodshed on the island. It was hard to realize. The glorious lonely line of snows breathed peace instead of war.

Marseilles is busy and bustling and I won't keep you long with me there. I wish, though, that I could take you high up on the hill to the church of Notre Dame de la Garde, where there is a splendid wide view over the sea, as fine a view as you will find in all the Riviera. I'd like, too, to have you stop in quaint Avignon so we could wander in the narrow streets, where the walls almost nod together, and visit the palace of the popes, and see the old bridge of Avignon, famous in French nursery rhyme, where the people used to dance and dance.

But on to Paris, where we devoted ourselves seriously to frills and furbelows.

Paterfamilias and the Wise One had gone straight to Paris from Lyons, leaving me to run over to Switzerland for a visit with old friends there. It was in that wise that I traveled alone from Geneva to Paris, quite a l'Américaine, having for traveling companions a chic and charming Parisenne, and a rather vinegary young Swiss girl. It is a night's ride, and the principal interruption to our slumbers was the clatter and bang of the long, flat metal water cans that are slid at intervals in and out of the railway carriages. They are filled with hot water and are removed as soon as the water gets cold. They lie along the floor under one's feet and are the only means of heating provided, consequently passengers on a night train in France are more or less bulbous bundles of woolen rugs. The sleeping cars are very unsatisfactory, and one travels more comfortably in the ordinary first-class carriages.

At 7 o'clock we were in the metropolis, the only city in the world to every Frenchman.

Due West Again

The morning was wet and soggy and cross. All Paris was under an umbrella. Hailing one of the weather-beaten coachmen that are to be secured any where in the city by the raising of a finger (consideration, one franc fifty with *pourboire*), I climbed into the ramshackle little carriage and rolled away, contented as a warm cat to be back in Paris—Paris, the charming, the beautiful, in rain or shine.

There is no poor quarter in the city, apparently. You find the same broad, well-kept streets and boulevards, the same rows of handsome, uniform buildings wherever you go. This is explained by the fact that poor and rich live under the same roof, and, generally speaking, there is no separate business and residence quarter. The Rue de la Chaussée d' Antin, for instance, one of the busiest and most crowded thoroughfares in Paris, is the street in which many wealthy merchants and bankers live. As you walk along the street you would think it entirely given over to business, but an occasional glimpse through a broad doorway will reveal an elaborately decorated court; or, perhaps, from another door, flanked by the establishments of the butcher and baker, an elegant carriage will emerge, with coachman and footman outside and Madame inside, arrayed in silks and laces ready for a promenade in the Bois.

But let me see, we were rattling along in a modest fiacre from the Gare de Lyon. Here is the Place de la Bastille, at the end of the "big boulevards," where the Bastille formerly stood. It is wet and misty, and the tall, bronze July column, with its winged figure so lightly poised, glistens like polished marble. Across the open square a group of little French school-boys are running on their way to school. They look like hobgoblins, with the peaked hood of their circulars pulled up over their heads, and their bare knees peeping out above their stockings. It is a fantastic Paris this morning. A heavy omnibus, drawn by three perfectly matched Norman horses, is rumbling by, and the dark figures on top, crouching under umbrellas, look like a growth of weird toadstools.

And now we are threading our way along the "big boulevards," with their multiplicity of signs, and, at this hour of the morning, their streams of hurrying, businesslike pedestrians. In the afternoon the very atmosphere of the boulevards will be changed. Paris will be joyous and sauntering, particularly so if it be sunny. To see the boulevards at their happiest, you should be here in carnival time, when the trees are festooned with myriads of fluttering paper ribbons, and the air is filled with a gay shower of rainbow-colored confetti. The boulevards are carpeted with the tiny circles of vari-colored paper, and every one makes merry.

Just now there is more than a hint of spring in the air. Ever since we entered France our eyes have been refreshed by the verdure, so doubly welcome after dusty Egypt and dustier India. In the Bois, or Bois de Boulogne (Woods of Boulogne), to give it the full title, the buds have burst into tiny leaves of that sweet, fresh, tender green that the French call primevert. We seem to have no word for the first virgin color of the spring.

Due West Again

Ah, I have sometimes wavered a little in my loyalty to Paris as the most beautiful city in the world when I have been traveling elsewhere, but I always reproach myself for it when I get back again. Surely, there is not so beautiful a square on the globe as the wide, stately Place de la Concorde, so inappropriately named the Place of Peace, for in the days of the Commune, not so long ago, it bristled with cannon, and long before that, at the time of the Reign of Terror, the dread guillotine stood in the center, where an obelisk now stands, between two splashing fountains. In that black time more than two thousand people were guillotined and a sewer had to be built to carry their blood to the Seine.

The Place de la Concorde is so smiling now, so characteristic of this rubber ball of a Paris that always rebounds from misfortune and quickly wipes away the traces of war and bloodshed. On one side is the Rue Royale, and at the end of the street you can see the massive columns of the Church of the Madeleine, Napoleon's Temple of Glory. To the right are the Gardens of the Tuileries, where the beauty of nature has been allowed to replace the ruins of the burned palace. Opposite the Rue Royale is the bridge of La Concorde, and beyond the Seine, the Chamber of Deputies. From the bridge looking up and down the river, you can see on one side the soaring Eiffel tower and the minarets of the Trocadero which recall the mosque of Mahomet Ali in Cairo; in the other direction, the galleries and Palace of the Louvre. Farther on are the twin towers of Notre Dame and the slender spire of the Sainte Chapelle.

One Way Round the World

It is a noble array of edifices. If one could only see the gossamer threads of a hundred histories that are woven in the air.

It takes little imagination to think of active, busy, seething Paris as a being endowed with life, and the swirling stream that flows through the Place de la Concorde seems to be its very heart beat.

The noblest approach of all is the Avenue des Champs Elysées. Far up at the end of its gentle slope you see a misty little arch, that frames a bit of the sky, and seems set on the very edge of the horizon. As you drive up the avenue, between the rows of trees and flower beds, past the Rond Point with its fountains, along with the crowd of well-dressed cosmopolitan pedestrians and elegant turnouts, the diminutive arch grows and widens till it becomes the beautiful Arc de Triomphe, the splendid monument of the great Napoleon's victories that the world admires.

There is ever something to do in Paris. Sometimes it is to stroll in the Latin quarter, as did the famous three musketeers of the brush, sometimes to wander in the museums and palaces, sometimes to sit at a little table in front of one of the big cafés of the boulevards watching the gay boulevardiers stroll by, gotten up regardless as J. M. would say, sometimes to go to the opera, the theater, for a drive in the Bois. The praise of the French woman's taste has been almost over-sung, but for an air of spruceness and general well-grooming a well-dressed Frenchman can challenge the world. Not that I would place him ahead of the American in effect.

Due West Again

It is only that his dapperness is striking. There are the poor too on the boulevards. Elegance rubs elbows with misery in the most beautiful city in the world as it does everywhere.

There is no denying that we were very frivolous, very Frenchy as we say (very American, the French say for the same thing), in our choice of amusements. Paterfamilias does not understand French so he enjoys an entertainment where there is a charm of light and color, and froth of that sort is plentiful. At the Scala we saw Yvette Guilbert and were charmed by her genius. Her work glows with that rare quality and she redeems an indelicacy that is inevitable in French music halls.

At the Folies Bergère we saw Otéro, the Spanish beauty and incidentally the Spanish dancer. She is a celebrity and she blazes with jewels, but she lacks magnetism and we didn't care for her. She is a radiant picture, however, in a gown of shimmering satin that glitters with gems. Her throat and arms and hands are covered with them, and they sparkle in the embroidery of her bodice and skirt. We liked better "Kara, the great American (?) juggler," who skillfully juggled with everything he could lay hands on, including the newspapers, tables, billiard balls, cues in a café and finally the waiter himself.

Would it interest you, I wonder, to know how I renewed acquaintance at the Folies Bergère, with my friend, Mr. Jack Horne? Truth is really stranger than fiction and I leave it to you if, in a story book, such a meeting would not be a strain on one's credulity.

One Way Round the World

Mr. Jack Horne is an Australian whom we had met a number of times in Japan and China, and we saw him last in Hong-Kong, as we were sailing for Singapore. If he told me his plans I had forgotten them and we had drifted in different directions and lost sight of one another. That night as I sat at the Folies Bergère, my eyes wandered over the audience, a glowing one by the way, for Paris is ablaze with red, and there sitting in one of the open boxes, just one removed from ours, was Mr. Jack Horne. That we were mutually surprised goes without saying. Mr. Horne had come around on the other side of the world, by Japan and America, while I had come by India and Egypt, and we found ourselves in almost adjoining boxes in Paris at the Folies Bergère.

. . . .

Let me tell you a joke on the French! Their motto, as you know, is Liberté, Egalité, Fraternité, liberty, equality, fraternity for all. One day as we were riding on top of an omnibus out to Père la Chaise Cemetery, my eye was caught by the familiar words carved in stone over the gateway of La Roquette Prison. It is in front of this gateway that you see the flagstones in the pavement on which the guillotine is set up, and don't you think it a delicious satire that they should have chosen to decorate the grim entrance of a prison, which occasionally looks down on a guillotine, with Liberty, Equality, Fraternity?

. . . .

London was all agog with excitement over the prepara-

ONE OF LANDSEER'S LIONS

Due West Again

tions for the Jubilee. Trafalgar Square was busier than ever and Landseer's splendid lions at the foot of the Nelson monument stood out with an added touch of repose and majesty. Neither had the commotion invaded Westminster Abbey. It was lofty and peaceful and silent, full of association and inspiration.

But London had no charms for Paterfamilias on this occasion. Acute nostalgia had seized him. We found him interested only in packing and steamers and home going. Aided and abetted by Mr. P. he changed our date of sailing only three times, each time for an earlier one. The Wise One and I thought it good form to demur but at heart we were not unwilling. Mr. P. is an old and valued friend who traveled with Paterfamilias and the Wise One several years ago in Mexico. His path had crossed ours again in Paris and he has shared our fortunes since. The man who finds the world oppressively small is the man who has a reason to want to get away, but for people with comparatively clear consciences the sight of familiar faces in unfamiliar places is as cool water is to thirst.

· · · · · · · ·

We were on board the Normannia for our last voyage toward the west. It gives one an odd sensation to leave his country at San Francisco and come back to it at New York. There is a wide journey between them, a voyage of great discovery, and "east or west home's best."

New York harbor was in gala dress. The White Squadron lay in the bay ready to take part in the ceremony at the unveiling of General Grant's monument. I've been lately entertained by the clever observations of a London newspaper man, who enclosed his opinions of us between the covers of a very red book and called it "The Land of the Dollar." On entering New York he was most impressed by the advertisements for Castoria, which, it must be confessed, spring up there as thick as brown-eyed Susans along a Hoosier rail fence. He did not know what Castoria was. "It appears that children cry for it," he observed, "which seems a poor enough recommendation to the harassed parent." We ignored the Castoria signs and waxed enthusiastic over New York's beauties as we pointed them out to our French and German companions. "Hooray!" we telegraphed, "we're here," and in another twenty-four hours or two Paterfamilias, the Wise One and I had put a period to our pilgrimage at our own fireside.

Greetings! my friends, the arm-chair travelers, who have followed me in my wanderings, perhaps toasting your toes at the fender while I screened myself from a blazing tropical sun, perhaps fanning yourselves with palm leaves while I shivered on mountain tops—may your journeys be as pleasant and your lives long, and so good-bye!